Presidential Character:

George Washington-John Quincy Adams

Darrell,
Hope you
enjoy!
Tim
Hebbler

Presidential Character

George Washington-John Quincy Adams

TIMOTHY D. HOLDER

A look at the first six presidents' views on

faith, race, and leadership

Copyright © 2015 by
TDH Communications
Knoxville, TN

Cover art by
Steve Ellis
Light House Studio
Knoxville, TN

DEDICATION

To Jonathon Hodge, a lover of history, a man of faith, a friend to all,
and a leader of many...

ACKNOWLEDGEMENTS

Dr. Chad Gregory, a History professor at Tri-County Technical College, was a tremendous asset on this project. His background in American religious history enabled him to provide many interesting insights and helpful comments. The benefit he was to this project greatly outweighs the cost of the steak dinner I hope to someday buy him as a token of my thanks for his efforts.

I appreciated the time taken by the scholars I interviewed for *Presidential Character*. Drs. Charles N. Edel, Randall O'Brien, W. Brian Shelton, and Mary V. Thompson were generous with their comments and a pleasure to work with.

Steve Ellis of Light House Studio has always done great work with cover art, and this book has been no exception. He is a true professional and his friendship is a blessing.

I am thankful for my parents, Charles and Judy Holder, and my in-laws, Jack and Carol Easterday, and their overwhelming love and support.

Mary Ruth McNatt has been a wellspring of encouragement over the years. Her belief in me has been and continues to be an inspiration.

I owe a hearty thank you to Bill Brown for doing a little market research and for setting a great example of doing the right things the right way.

Though this book bears little resemblance to the paper that spawned it, I am appreciative of the input of two Religion professors at Carson-Newman University who reviewed my thesis. Dr. Andrew Smith provided input on matters too numerous to count. Dr. Mel Hawkins stressed the importance of primary documents, which resulted in a greater reliance on them than would otherwise be the case.

Anything of note that I have accomplished over the last several years has been accompanied by the support and encouragement of my wonderful wife, Dr. Angela Easterday Holder. It is not just that I love her; I admire her, too.

TABLE OF CONTENTS

Chapter 1. Introduction.. 10

Chapter 2. Faith and Slavery.. 19

Chapter 3. George Washington...35

Chapter 4. John Adams... 51

Chapter 5. Thomas Jefferson...66

Chapter 6. James Madison.. 83

Chapter 7. James Monroe...97

Chapter 8. John Quincy Adams..111

Chapter 9. Conclusions.. 126

Appendix: About the Sources.. 132

Sources..139

CHAPTER 1

INTRODUCTION

Hopefully, general readers will find this book to be, one might say, generally readable, but the intention here was to write something academically worthwhile as well as personally enjoyable. This is a book about the early presidents, filled with interesting stories and information, but it is also more than that. In an effort to satisfy academic considerations, many notations were included, primary writings were used, and there is a section in the back describing the sources.[1]

The book you are reading is about the faith, views on race, and leadership of the first six presidents. This leads to two quite logical questions: Why write a book combining a study of faith, views on race, and leadership; and why would one choose to focus on the first six presidents?

My manuscript actually started as a study of the religious views of early presidents from the South. This served as the thesis for a

---

[1] There is one exception I am making to academic convention. Because I have cited so many other writers in this book, I will use the first person when referring to myself, rather than confusing the issue with references to "the author."

Master's degree in Applied Theology at Carson-Newman University. My intent all along was to take the thesis and turn it into some kind of book, but the original vision changed over time. As I researched faith in the early American South, I was fascinated by the issue of slavery. What role did religion play regarding this institution? Some people attacked slavery with faith-based arguments, but others used the Bible to defend it.[2] Both sides easily found ammunition for their cause. The Bible says one should treat others the way one wants to be treated, and it also encourages believers to love each other, neighbors, strangers, and enemies, which seems to cover just about everybody.[3] But this same Bible also teaches that slaves should obey their masters, and these masters rather than freeing their slaves, should simply treat them fairly.[4]

Looking at both faith and African American relations is relevant today in America. As society has become more secularized, people sometimes discuss the proper role of religion, and they debate what role it played historically. Also given the racial tensions in Ferguson, Missouri in 2014-2015 and other places, looking at part of the history of racial issues in America seems relevant, too. The other side of that coin, though, is the reality that the United States has gone from being a country where African Americans were owned as property to having a two-term, African American president. It is important to note how far we have come.[5]

Finally, this book deals with leaders—how they thought, what they said, and what they did—so insights on leadership were difficult to ignore. The men studied here share some similarities, and they reached the highest office in the land, but their strengths and their methods were quite distinct from one another.

This brings us to the issue of the number of presidents. As stated above, my thesis covered early southern presidents. I looked at ten men from number one—George Washington, of course—through

---

[2] One can find examples of this in Joseph J. Ellis' *Founding Brothers* (New York: Vintage Books, 2000), 85-86.

[3] See Luke 6:31, Mark 12:31, Luke 10:25-37, and Luke 6:27.

[4] Colossians 3:23 and 4:1.

[5] It should be noted that even though the term "race" is used, I am really just focusing on African Americans. I did not want to make my study too broad.

number seventeen, Andrew Johnson. But for this book, there was really no compelling reason to skip over anyone—there was no reason to just focus on one geographical region of the country. I did not want to do so many presidents that the book lacked depth, thus, I decided to cover from Washington through James K. Polk. The more the more in-depth the study became, though, the more I realized that I wanted to focus on an even smaller number of presidents, so I narrowed my scope to its final form. Perhaps another volume of presidents will appear in a few years.

One of the upsides to just covering the first six presidents is that they all knew each other.[6] The world they faced was rapidly changing, but there were commonalities to their issues that are lost when one covers too broad a stretch of time.

Was America a Christian land in want of Christian leaders, or was there a different dynamic at work? Depending on whom you read, George Washington was a "devout believer in Jesus Christ," and he had a "fervent evangelical faith." Or, by the standards of "twenty-first century evangelical Christianity—Washington was not a Christian."[7] Historian Joseph J. Ellis describes the first president as "a lukewarm Episcopalian."[8] Given what the Bible has to say about being lukewarm,[9] what does that tell the reader about Washington's faith? Ellis also writes that Washington was "never a deeply religious man, at least not in the traditional Christian sense of the term," and that "Washington thought of God as a distant, impersonal force." Where did Washington really stand? Was he a misunderstood skeptic, was he a spiritually-indifferent politician who offered religious platitudes to placate the masses, or was he a man of faith who has been misrepresented over time?

---

[6] They did not always like each other, but they were well-acquainted.

[7] The first two quotations were from Tim LaHaye and D. James Kennedy, respectively. The third was from Steven Waldman, and all of them are found in his book *Founding Faith* (New York: Random House, 2008), 56, 60.

[8] Joseph J. Ellis, *His Excellency: George Washington* (New York: Alfred A. Knopf, 2004) 45, 151, 269.

[9] Hint: it is not nice—it involves vomit. Revelation 3:15-16

The first president is not the only Christian question mark among our early chief executives. Acclaimed historian David McCullough calls John Adams "a devout Christian," but Steven Waldman considers the second president an "angry Unitarian."[10] John Adams once referred to himself as "a churchgoing animal," but did a passion for worship services mean he was a Christian? And who was Thomas Jefferson? Was he a man with a Christian worldview whose beliefs have been covered up and explained away by anti-Christian scholars, or was he a heretic who cut the miracle stories out of his Bible?

With such differing opinions on these men and the three that followed them, what are we to believe?

Many books have been written on the faith of the presidents, but the debates continue. There are rather secular-minded historians who have a tendency to downplay the religiosity of the Founders, and evangelical Christians who seem to overstate the presidents' faith. I have a foot in both worlds with a Ph. D. and a Master's in History, but also a Master's degree in Applied Theology and a BA in Bible. As a Christian, I am sympathetic to the evangelical position, but as a historian I am content to go where the evidence takes me. Whether or not, for example, James Madison was a Christian does not really impact the role of faith in America today, or in my own life, so I have no conscious agenda based on proving such an argument. The truth might be inconvenient, to paraphrase Al Gore; but it can also set one free, according to an earlier authority. My goal is to get to the truth of what was happening back then by sharing pertinent information about these men and telling interesting stories.

It should be noted that these presidents will not be getting equal attention on faith-related questions primarily because they did not provide the same amount of relevant material for historians. James Monroe, for example, gave posterity little to work with regarding his religious views. In and of itself this tells us something—if Monroe had been a pious man there should be evidence of it, given his many years

---

[10] David McCullough *John Adams* (New York: Touchstone Book, 2002), 19. Waldman, vii.

in the national spotlight. Admittedly, when Monroe's wife died, he was so stricken with grief that he burned the lifetime of letters they had sent to each other, so any hints as to Monroe's theology contained therein were lost forever.[11] Nevertheless, if he had been serious about his faith there should be evidence of it from his public statements and from what his contemporaries had to say about him.

A trip to Mount Vernon reveals that Martha Washington burned much of her husband's correspondence after his death, too.[12] But there is still a great deal of evidence today of what George Washington had to say and do regarding religion. As our first and trendsetting president, whatever he offered was highly scrutinized. Washington tended to avoid the finer points of theology, but he wrestled with the broader subject enough that Mary V. Thompson was able to devote an entire book to a balanced and thorough study of his faith.[13]

Determining the religious views of these presidents is complicated by many things. One cannot really *know* what thoughts someone held most dear some two hundred years ago. As a result sometimes too much is read into a specific quotation or event with the assumption that it represents the totality of a person. Sometimes people go through radical changes in their beliefs and values, thus a statement or action at one point in time might not be reflective of where they ended up theologically. It is also worth mentioning that Americans in this era frequently quoted the Bible because it was so commonly read. Whereas today biblical quotations are often associated with the devout, back then such an action might simply be an attempt to relate to the general public by citing the familiar.

Insight into these men is also made difficult by the fact that they were politicians—some of them, like Thomas Jefferson, more calculating than others, but all politicians—so they played to the crowd.

---

[11] Harlow Giles Unger, *The Last Founding Father* (Philadelphia: Da Capo Press, 2009), 343.

[12] Parenthetically, some believe that Thomas Jefferson did the same thing with his correspondence with his wife. Jon Meacham *Thomas Jefferson* (New York: Random House, 2012), 89-90.

[13] Mary V. Thompson, *In the Hands of a Good Providence* (Charlottesville: University of Virginia Press, 2008).

They were concerned about how they would be remembered by history. Also, because they were politicians, they were magnets for labels. Supporters of Jefferson might call him a Christian to placate the faithful while critics sometimes called the man an atheist to mobilize forces against him. In both cases, the labels could have been a means to an end more so than an insightful look into the state of the third president's soul.

One question that has to be wrestled with when talking about faith is what does a specific label mean? For example, what is a functional definition of what it means to be a Christian? Different claims are made today and back then about how to define the term. Christian theologian W. Brian Shelton says, "A Christ follower is any adherent to the teaching of Jesus who professes belief in the resurrected Lord and who acts according to a model of Christian discipleship."[14]

Obviously, many can claim that their views and actions are Christian without that being the case. Within this era of study, orthodox Christianity faced challenges from people who called themselves Christians and who were quite religious, but whose views contradicted a fair reading of Scripture. Deists and Unitarians fall into this category.

Shelton describes Deism as "a religious worldview emphasizing the existence and creation of a Christian God who does not engage or interact providentially in that creation."[15] Deists believed that there was some kind of Creator-God who formed the universe but was no longer involved in it. Miracles were not real; Jesus was not divine. God created the universe to function on its own, like a watchmaker who creates a timepiece that functions independently of his efforts. Additionally, Deists held that Christianity with its flawed elevation of Christ was not necessarily superior to the other religions of the world. While the historian David L. Holmes considers George Washington to be a Christian Deist, as opposed to being a non-Christian Deist or an orthodox Christian, there are those who do not recognize such a distinction. The colonial era, Puritan theologian Jonathan Edwards felt he had nothing in common with Deists because they denied the deity of

---

[14] Shelton interview—April 19, 2015.
[15] Ibid.

Christ, the authority of the prophets and apostles, and the inspiration of Scripture.[16] Edwards felt that it was impossible to be both a Christian and a Deist, and longstanding orthodoxy is on his side.

Peter Marshall and David Manuel describe the difference between Deism and Unitarianism. "Unitarianism was a close neighbor of Deism," they write, "for if there was one abstract God, then why not one benevolent, universal Intelligence, embodying love?"[17] Thus, Unitarians of that era tended to have warmer feelings toward God than Deists, who leaned more towards apathy.

When it comes to race, the facts seem straightforward enough, but maybe they do not tell the full story. Four of the first six presidents were slave owning southerners. The northerners, John Adams and John Quincy Adams, opposed the institution in word and deed.

Should Washington simply be dismissed as just another slave owner, or should he get credit for freeing over one hundred more slaves than Jefferson, who wrote "all men are created equal?" Should John Adams be praised for not owning slaves and held in high esteem for his remarks and actions against the institution, or criticized for once using the term "negroes" in a negative way?[18]

The equation seems easy enough: slave owner=very bad person, but history is more complicated than that. What would you do, dear reader, if you were born and raised in a culture where you inherited slaves? What if over time you came to see the institution as evil, and you wanted a way out, but you could not come up with a feasible plan, given the economic and legal realities you would have faced back then? Should Madison and Monroe get credit for trying desperately to create and implement such a plan, but failing? Were they better or worse than men and women who did not own slaves but were untroubled or indifferent to their suffering? Should any sympathy for the slave owner evaporate if even one rich southerner could come up with a system to free his slaves? One did. You will read about Robert Carter in the pages to come.

---

[16] Thompson, 2-4.

[17] Peter Marshall and David Manuel, *From Sea to Shining Sea* (Grand Rapids: Fleming H. Revell, 1986), 108-109.

[18] See chapter four for the story behind that.

Moving on from faith and race brings us to the final theme of this book: leadership. What does it mean to be a leader? What does it take? Basically, what did leadership look like, as embodied by the first six presidents?

Jon Meacham says, "Jefferson hungered for greatness,"[19] and really the same could be said of the others, too. All six of these men were ambitious, but was that a bad thing? President Warren G. Harding once said, "Ambition is a commendable attribute without which no man succeeds. Only inconsiderate ambition imperils." Of course, Harding might not be the best arbiter of what is commendable, given his own, quite considerable character issues.[20]

A different kind of chief executive, President Randall O'Brien of Carson-Newman University, offers an interesting take on ambition. He says, "I'm not power hungry, but I am impact hungry. I want to make a difference."[21] The six studied here all wanted to make an impact on history; they wanted their lives to matter on some level that was bigger than themselves.

These six men all rose to the number one leadership position in the country, but they hardly did it the same way. Washington was a war general. Adams was a shrewd and zealous politician. Jefferson was a genius with words, and he was a charmer. Madison was a brilliant man who formed a series of shrewd alliances with several of the most significant Founders, even though those men did not always see eye to eye with each other.[22] Monroe was a war hero and a smart and charismatic politician. John Quincy Adams was an extraordinary diplomat. Finally, as stated above, they were all tirelessly ambitious.

Assessing the leadership of these men has to include in part perceptions of them by their contemporaries. Did the citizenry and their fellow politicians see them as good leaders? Part of the challenge here is that these men served over many years and perceptions change.

---

[19] Jon Meacham, *Thomas Jefferson* (New York: Random House, 2012), xxviii.

[20] Perhaps I will delve into those in a later volume.

[21] Interview with author, April 21, 2015.

[22] There is actually a whole book devoted to Madison's alliance with his fellow Virginian George Washington. Stuart Leibiger, *Founding Friendship* (Charlottesville: University of Virginia Press, 2001).

Some traits might lead to success in one area but failure in another. Some issues might turn out great, but others prove too difficult to overcome, thus impacting perceptions of a given president. Consider George W. Bush, whose approval rating after his early handling of 9/11 was over 80%. By the time he left office, it was under 30%. This is an extreme example, but all presidents experience peaks and valleys. Focusing too much on just one gives a false overall impression.

George Washington is the only president in American history to be elected unanimously by the Electoral College, but James Monroe was almost as impressive. In his re-election bid, the fifth president received every Electoral vote that was cast, except one. A modern reader might be tempted to think this would demonstrate that Monroe was almost Washington's equal as a leader. But did climbing to such rarified air actually prove to be Monroe's undoing?

Some of these men, as you shall read, might have been victims of the Peter Principle—which is a term describing the unfortunate circumstance of a person rising above his or her level of competence.

Conveniently, these six men had similarities in their outlook on party politics that set them apart from every president that came after them, according to Ralph Ketcham's *Presidents above Party*. The six saw political parties as a bad thing for America,[23] though what they did based on that mindset varied, as we shall see.

Moving forward, chapter two will give some background on faith and slavery in early America. The chapters after that will cover the first six presidents individually. At the end, there will be a chapter regarding conclusions followed by a chapter on the sources, and finally, a comprehensive listing of the sources themselves.

Thank you for reading.

---

[23] Ralph Ketcham, *Presidents above Party* (Chapel Hill: University of North Carolina Press, 1984), xi.

CHAPTER 2

FAITH AND SLAVERY

We can better understand the first six presidents if we know something about the culture from which they sprang. This chapter deals specifically with faith and slavery in the English colonies and in the early days of the republic. People tend to think of Massachusetts, home of the Pilgrims, as the one religion-based location, but churches were strong throughout the colonies. And religion played a major role on both sides of the slavery issue.

If one's interests as a reader are more tightly focused just on the six men themselves, feel free to skip ahead to the next chapter.

When Alexis de Tocqueville was visiting America in the early 1800s, he sat next to John Quincy Adams at dinner one night. Adams told him that the key to understanding the United States was to remember that, as Adams biographer Charles N. Edel describes the conversation, "The Puritans explained the North, and slavery the South."[24] It was actually a little more complicated than that, but maybe not by much.

Europeans arriving in the New World in this era came from a society where church and state were connected. These two institutions naturally fit together because they shared priorities: protect the people from outside threats, either spiritual or earthly, and make sure order was maintained within the realm by encouraging people to get along

---

[24] Charles N. Edel, *Nation Builder* (Cambridge MA: Harvard University Press, 2014), 260.

with their neighbors. More cynically, those in power colluded in reinforcing the idea of submission to authority.

The relationship between church and state that was so prevalent in Europe became the norm in many English colonies in America, too. The Puritans went from being an oppressed minority in England to oppressing other religious minorities in Massachusetts; and early Virginian Anglicans, who are not often remembered for their religiosity, were guilty of the same sin—that of trying to quash any diversity in religious thought.

The first group of successful English settlers in America founded the Virginia colony in 1607, and they did not consist of pilgrims like the later Massachusetts Bay Colony. But a strict religious structure was quickly imposed in Virginia by 1611 to help colonists cope with their harsh environment. This Anglican brand of Christianity was concerned less with a personal relationship with Jesus than with rules, traditions, and a comforting sense of community, according to historian Donald Mathews.[25] These rules were quickly relaxed to a degree, but the trend in Virginia, Massachusetts, and most of the other colonies was for the governing body to endorse and try to enforce adherence to one sect of Christianity. There were established churches, meaning a specific church that was taxpayer-supported, in nine of the original thirteen colonies. [26]

State religion did not have an easy time of it though. Diverse populations from several European nations settling within individual colonies made it difficult for a single Protestant denomination to hold sway. For the Dutch who populated New York,[27] the German Quakers who moved to Pennsylvania, etc., there was little interest in embracing the English Church. Another problem for the Puritans in Massachusetts and the Anglicans elsewhere was the sheer vastness of the geography that existed. Isolated families and communities were free to abandon

---

[25] Donald Mathews, *Religion in the Old South* (Chicago: University of Chicago Press, 1977), 1-4.
[26] David L. Holmes, *The Faiths of the Founding Fathers* (New York: Oxford University Press, 2006), 9.
[27] It was called new Netherlands before the English took it over and changed the name.

their religion or get creative in its practice. Finally, as will be covered below, Anglicanism might have held control of the people longer in many of the colonies were it not for some significant flaws within the American branch of the Anglican Church itself.

In these early days, there were many sects competing for souls, including Anglicans, Congregationalists (which is what the Puritans were more formally known as), Baptists, Methodists, Presbyterians, Catholics, Unitarians, Deists, and others.

A surprisingly large number in the South in particular basically made up their own religions.[28] For example, wealthy Virginia planter Robert Carter III went from being an Anglican to a Baptist to a Swedenborgian. When Carter soured on Swedenborg, he visited the Quakers, but that did not work for him either, so he tried to create his own congregation of Swedenborgians. When this effort failed, Carter's "travels on the spiritual plane turned chaotic."[29]

The Quakers are often assumed to have been primarily confined to Pennsylvania, and indeed they were strong there, but they had a greater presence in colonial America as a whole than many people realize. The Religious Society of Friends, as Quakers are more properly known, existed in large numbers in the South, and as early as the seventeenth century, they were making inroads among all classes of people.[30] David L. Holmes estimates that the Quakers were the fifth largest sect among colonial churches and existed in significant numbers in Virginia and North Carolina.[31]

Ben Franklin was no southern planter. Actually, he was originally from the same state as John Adams—Massachusetts. Franklin was also a leader in colonial society, and he provides the reader with a fascinating example of the creative theology at work in

---

[28] Christine L. Heyrman, *Southern Cross* (Chapel Hill: North Carolina Press, 1997), 208-209.

[29] Emmanuel Swedenborg had founded something called the Church of the New Jerusalem. Andrew Levy, *The First Emancipator: Slavery, Religion, and the Quiet Resolution of Robert Carter* (New York: Random House, 2005), 114, 164-165.

[30] Edmund S. Morgan, *American Slavery—American Freedom* (New York: W.W. Norton & Company, 1975), 374.

[31] Holmes, 5.

this time and place. Franklin is usually described by historians as a Deist, but his beliefs were more exotic than that. In Franklin's "Articles of Belief and Acts" he affirmed his belief in the existence of a Supreme Being, but he also went on to speculate that there were many other beings that were set in place somewhere between God and humanity, and it is one of these other "Beings or Gods," as Franklin wrote, "who is the Author and owner of our (solar) system."[32]

There was a good deal of diversity and genuine tension even among the orthodox Christians. The Congregationalist/Puritan Church actually became the breeding ground for the original Unitarians in Massachusetts. Baptists, Methodists, and Presbyterians—the evangelical denominations—demanded penitent, adult decisions to follow Christ. In contrast to the passion in which these evangelicals exulted, Anglicans typically cultivated a more sedate faith experience. Rather than the emotional stories of penitent adults that epitomized the evangelical experience, Anglicans believed that as long as they were christened as babies and partook of Communion at some point as adults then their Christian faith was both real and evident. It bears mentioning that in a culture where life was hard and death a frequent companion, a degree of stoicism was quite useful,[33] even admired. When one tried to keep a stiff upper lip because of the difficulties of life, why act differently in church? Anglicans tended to not be impressed by the emotionalism of the evangelicals.

Whereas the modern reader might infer that a passionate faith was a more genuine version, for many Anglicans this passion brought more alarm than admiration. Some of those who responded to the evangelical message were so overcome with guilt over their sinfulness that it literally pushed them to the brink of sanity and beyond. After seeing the extremes to which some of the penitent were driven, others in their community wanted to protect themselves and their loved ones from such a dangerous theology.[34]

---

[32] Alf J. Mapp, Jr., *The Faiths of our Founders* (New York: Fall River Press, 2006), 24-25.
[33] Heyrman, 39, 44-45.
[34] Ibid., 32-36.

In the North, the Congregationalist Church was in control in Massachusetts, but some people who did not want to pay taxes to the Puritans' church or otherwise submit to a Puritan-dominated colonial government. Some of these dissenters left and founded Connecticut and Rhode Island.

In the South, the Anglican Church had the upper hand. This establishment of the Anglicans happened in Virginia in 1632 and in the Carolinas by 1706.[35] The Virginia government originally had the Quakers in mind when the legislature made it a crime to not baptize children into the Anglican faith.[36] Because the Anglicans had the support of the colonial authorities in the South, evangelical preachers would occasionally be fined for not attending the local Anglican Church and for preaching publicly without Anglican credentials.[37]

Enforcement of religious-based laws was inconsistent given the vast amount of wide open spaces in the seventeenth century, but there was little doubt what the preferences of the colonial authorities were. A series of laws were passed in Virginia from the 1620s until the 1660s with several of them specifically targeting Baptists and Quakers. Some Baptists responded by crossing the border into North Carolina. [38]

Sentiment was such in the Virginia Assembly that one member was expelled from that body because his colleagues considered him guilty of being "loving to Quakers."[39]

Despite their advantage, the Anglican clergy in Virginia were in a precarious situation in the 1700s. In most cases they had emigrated from England, so they lacked a base of family and friends in America. These clergymen needed the support of the local community leaders—a planter class that prided itself on its individuality and independence. The planters tended to be disgusted by weakness, which they often perceived in the poorly-paid, poorly-connected Anglican priests. The

---

[35] Mathews, 3.

[36] Jon Meacham, *American Gospel* (New York: Random House, 2007), 58.

[37] Mathews, 16.

[38] Sydney E. Ahlstrom, *A Religious History of the American People*, Volume 1, (Garden City, NY: Image Books, 1975), 246-247.

[39] Ibid.

priests agitated for higher salaries and more security whereas the gentry thought that more piety was a better remedy for the priests' concerns.[40]

Interestingly, the Anglican priests might have faced some disrespect from the rich and powerful, but the religious leaders nevertheless tried to relate to this class more than any other. The clergy shared the planters' typical disdain for the lower classes, and in return the lower classes often felt little warmth towards their priests.[41]

In addition to low pay and little respect, priests were frustrated by their chronic shortage of manpower, charged as they were with ministering to a widely dispersed population. Under these circumstances, Anglican pastors seemed helpless compared to the dissenting (evangelical) preachers that roamed the land.[42]

The colonies were under the authority of an English Parliament-mandated Act of Toleration, which should have opened the door for any Christian sect, but too many of those in charge in the colonies preferred maintaining the social order rather than scrupulously following the letter of the law. If people could challenge the religious (Anglican) teachings of a colony, whose authority would they *not* feel free to challenge? The situation was upset further by the First Great Awakening.[43] Perhaps the most popular of the Great Awakening preachers was George Whitefield, who came to America in 1740. He was an Anglican, but he was also an evangelical who preached that other Anglican clergy should not be trusted unless they showed evidence of a conversion experience. Other popular preachers echoed this theme.[44]

Arguing much along the same lines as Whitefield, revivalists like Gilbert Tennent in Pennsylvania said that sound doctrine was not enough for salvation if it was not accompanied by a personal conversion experience.[45]

---

[40] Rhys Isaac, *The Transformation of Virginia* (Chapel Hill: UNC Press, 1982), 144-145, 156.
[41] Mathews, 8-9.
[42] Ibid., 5-6.
[43] Isaac, 148, 152-153.
[44] Mathews, 13-14.
[45] Ahlstrom, Volume 1, 336.

The impact of Whitefield and the others was not as great in the South as it was in the New England and Middle Colonies, but other men followed. Sydney D. Ahlstrom refers to the First Great Awakening in the South as more of "an immense missionary enterprise than a revival," indicating that the South did not start out as the Bible Belt it would one day become. However one describes it, the floodgates were opening for other dissenting religious groups, much to the frustration of the Anglicans.[46]

The deterioration of Anglican control was exacerbated further by the reality that, as Rhys Isaac puts it, "A conception of priests as worldly extortioners was well established."[47]

Baptists continued to be persecuted into the 1770s, but they were becoming more and more popular, and they started fighting back, preaching against their political and priestly persecutors.[48] Thus, the authorities in Virginia continued to be quicker to arrest a Baptist preacher than apply the guidelines of the Act of Toleration.[49]

The earliest Virginian presidents sprang from a planter class subculture that liked the stability provided by an established religious sect even if this culture was uneasy with the clergy who ran the institution. The planters might have viewed the Anglican clergy as a mixed blessing at best, but the elites had more incentive to dislike the evangelicals. The Methodists, Baptists, and Presbyterians had a tendency to disrespect the established social order that was so rewarding to the planters and so cherished by many Anglican priests. Unfortunately for the evangelicals, they not only drew the wrath from the top of the social pyramid, but from the bottom as well. There are many stories of evangelical preachers being attacked physically by members of the lower classes. Donald Mathews describes the reason for this as a mystery, but he offers a likely, if partial, explanation. Women outnumbered the men in the evangelical churches, and some irreligious men were frustrated by the show of independence their wives displayed by getting involved in church.[50]

---

[46]Ahlstrom, Volume 1, 385-386.

[47] Isaac, 187.

[48] Ibid., 192-193.

[49] Heyrman, 200-201.

The Anglicans still held the advantage in their fight for religious control of the South. A point of tension between the planters and the evangelicals was that these planters enjoyed their status relative to their fellow men. They did not want to lose face by the perceived softness of churches that encouraged emotionalism, nor did they want to acknowledge a local, human authority higher than themselves, like a church disciplinary body. Also, churches that frowned on time spent in taverns and at cockfights threatened the recreations of many of the planters.[51] Jesus might have fraternized with tax collectors and sinners, but He never tax collected, nor sinned, a distinction many planters missed.

Sometimes the evangelicals struck back at the established church in less than spiritual ways. An Anglican missionary named Charles Woodmason had a hard time conducting services in South Carolina because local Presbyterians broke into his chapel and wiped excrement on his Communion table. They felt that the Anglican Communion rituals were too much like what one might find in a Catholic service.[52]

How religious were Americans in this era? Author Steven Waldman would not be considered a proponent of the Founders-as-evangelicals viewpoint, but when assessing the Continental Congress, Waldman writes, "Most public declarations simply assumed a Christian audience and vocabulary." In arguing his point, Waldman cites various references to God, Jesus Christ, and the Holy Ghost.[53]

After the Revolutionary War ended in the early 1780s, many Anglican priests went home to England. Their church in America collapsed. It would be reconstituted here by 1789 in the form of the Episcopal Church, but many former Anglicans drifted to other denominations. The Methodist Church was the biggest beneficiary of

---

[50] Mathews, 35-36, 102-104.

[51] Heyrman, 212-217.

[52] Ibid., 12.

[53] For example, he believes that George Washington was not a Christian by the standards of "twenty-first century conservative evangelical Christianity." Steven Waldman, *Founding Faith* (New York: Random House, 2008), 60, 71.

this shift, but the other evangelical churches in the South also saw substantial growth.

After the Anglican Church dissolved in America, evangelicals found themselves increasingly involved in the political system that had countenanced their persecution. Preachers, helped by a vocation that taught them how to express themselves well and think on their feet, began using the courts to their advantage. The evangelicals found themselves on the side of the law instead of being its victim.[54]

Evangelicals in Virginia greatly benefitted from the passage of the Statute for Religious Freedom by the state assembly in 1785. This law was championed by Thomas Jefferson and James Madison. When Virginia put together its state constitution in 1776, it weakened the Anglican Church's hold, but taxes for church support remained legal. The Statute for Religious Freedom struck that down. Interestingly, George Washington had not been as offended by this connection of government and religion as Jefferson and Madison were. Washington, who saw the practice of religion as important to the maintenance of an orderly society, was open to the idea of a middle ground between what Virginia had and what Jefferson and Madison wanted. Washington at one point suggested it might be a good idea to compel people to support a church, but let them pick which one, or if they were Jewish or Muslim they could be granted an exemption.[55]

Speaking of Jewish and Muslim worshipers, their needs were addressed when the Statute for Religious Freedom was being considered. As the legislators were hammering out the language of the statute, they looked at the phrase aimed at enforcing an established church. They included a line that read "coercion is a departure from the plan of the holy author of our religion." Someone suggested that Jesus Christ should be explicitly identified as the author of their religion, but this idea was voted down. According to Jefferson, this negative vote was an affirmation that the law was designed to protect "the Jew and the Gentile, the Christian and Mahometan, the Hindoo, and infidel of every denomination."[56]

---

[54] Heyrman, 240.

[55] Stuart Leibiger, *Founding Friendship* (Charlottesville: University of Virginia Press, 2001), 48-49.

When the Bill of Rights was ratified in 1791, it forbade the United States Congress from making any laws either supporting or hindering religion, but state governments were not affected by this federal constitutional commitment. It should also be noted that "even where legal constraints were absent, the social and economic preeminence of Episcopalians and Congregationalists was a challenge to" people of other faiths.[57] The United States was not technically a Christian nation because in accordance with the Constitution there was not an established church supported by the United States Government, nor was there a religious test to hold office. But the states were still greatly influenced by religion in the days of our earliest presidents.

Slavery was established early in the life of the colonies. Colonists started growing tobacco in Virginia in 1612. Land was aplenty, workers were needed, and indentured servitude seemed like an imperfect solution because the laborers earned their freedom after a fixed time of labor. A more permanent workforce was desired, and there was a thriving overseas slave trade already in operation. By 1619, slavers added the Virginia Colony to their list of stops. Because of slavery's early origin in colonies under British rule, some Americans would later find solace in blaming the Brits for imposing the peculiar institution on our country.

Massachusetts was spared the temptation of importing boatloads of slaves because the climate and soil were not conducive to big plantations that far north. Thus, John Adams and his son would encounter a handful of slaves in their home state, but the economic vitality of Massachusetts was never tied to slavery. It is always easier to be outraged by a vice that one does not find personally tempting.

Early on, the evangelicals frequently attacked the institution of slavery, but Heyrman notes that over time fewer and fewer preachers in the South seemed to have a problem with it. Heyrman observes a decrease in abolitionist rhetoric from 1760 to 1790. The Methodist

---

[56] Thomas Jefferson, *Memoir, Correspondence* (Alexandria, VA: Library of Alexandria, 2008). Kindle. L 785-794.
[57] Bernard A. Weisberger, *America Afire: Jefferson, Adams, and the Revolutionary Election of 1800* (New York: William Morrow, 2000), 35.

Church had sought to not allow slave owners to be members of their denomination, but church leaders had surrendered on this issue by around the time the Revolutionary War ended. Younger preachers kept up the fight longer, but even they made their peace with it in the South.[58]

In 1775, as revolutionary fever was seizing many of the colonists, the royal governor of Virginia threatened to free the slaves unless the colonists calmed themselves.[59] This was no idle threat. Many slaves were liberated in the South to undermine a war fought for liberty. It was a confusing time.

While critics of the Americans' history can correctly point out the hypocrisy of a fight for liberty ending in victory and continued slavery, there were serious blows struck against the institution decades before the Civil War pushed the issue to its resolution. The constitution of Massachusetts, which was written virtually single-handedly by John Adams, simply outlawed slavery in that state. In fairness, this was easier to do there than elsewhere because the slave population was already so small. Pennsylvania, where the abolitionist Quakers were so powerful, set in place a process and schedule for ending slavery even before the end of the Revolution. Other (but not all) northern states developed and implemented similar plans.

A possible reason for the decrease in rhetoric regarding abolitionism in the South in the late eighteenth century is that its success just seemed less likely. The number of slaves in the country increased from about 500,000 in 1776 to almost 700,000 at the time of the Census of 1790.[60]

There were several arguments made in favor of slavery. One, God had sanctioned it for the ancient Hebrews, so it was not wrong. Two, slavery was acceptable when it was used to guide an inferior race. According to this point of view, slavery was actually a burden for whites, but it was one they suffered for the good of a moral society. Three, the institution was good for white society—it was part of an economic system that would allow whites to enjoy material blessings.

---

[58] Heyrman, 26-27, 92-93, 138.
[59] Jon Meacham, *Thomas Jefferson* (New York: Random House), 81.
[60] Joseph J. Ellis, *Found Brothers* (New York: Vintage Books, 2000), 103.

It would be wrong to reject one of the Lord's blessings. Four, it was so ingrained in society that there was nothing evangelicals could do about it anyway.[61]

From the pro slavery point of view, the peculiar institution had rescued Africans from the evils of paganism and Islam, and life on the plantation was safer than it was in the factories that started springing up in the North later in the 1800s, so why were the abolitionists stirring up so much trouble? The point is that it was not clear cut in this era that to be a good Christian, one had to condemn slavery. Some Christians saw it as their duty to oppose the institution, but one could be devout and hold the position. People on both sides could argue extensively from Scripture and did. Despite the vehemence with which some argued against the peculiar institution, "manumission was never successfully identified as one of the marks of authentic conversion," according to Donald G. Mathews.[62]

That said, abolition was driven to a large degree by religious reformers. In fact, many abolitionists were not sure if politicians could be counted on to do more good than harm. There was some concern that politicians would be more apt to compromise on a moral issue that was too important to settle by half measures.[63]

While it might be tempting to say that slavery was simply too entrenched in the economy and the culture for the southern Founding Fathers to root it out single-handedly, this point of view ignores the story of Robert Carter. He was one of the richest slave owners in Virginia. Despite his political ambition, he sacrificed his personal goals for a greater good: he freed all of his slaves—more than four hundred total. He diversified his financial assets, sent his younger children to the North for their education so they would have greater exposure to abolitionist ideology, and set about preparing his slaves for the choices and responsibilities of freedom. Carter had to file paperwork and pay a fee to free each slave, according to state law, but he was willing, literally, to pay the price.[64] There was no way Carter could win an

---

[61] Mathews, 152.
[62] Ibid., 151.
[63] Norma Lois Peterson, *The Presidencies of William Henry Harrison and John Tyler* (Lawrence: University of Kansas, 1989), 3, 27.

election to public office after embarrassing the slave owning aristocracy by showing that it was possible to get out of massive slave ownership, but Carter sacrificed a political career for the greater good.

In the year 1790 the brand new US House of Representatives debated whether Congress should or could do something about slavery. The virulent response of southern politicians squelched much conversation until the aging Benjamin Franklin satirized one of the pro-slavery speeches given in the House. After a spirited back and forth, Congress shut down the debate and went mum on the subject, leaving abolitionist preachers to fight the good fight.[65] And so it remained for years.

A few years later, the Louisiana Purchase was partially negotiated by James Monroe and endorsed by then-President Thomas Jefferson. Thus, in the early 1800s the United States virtually doubled in size. This expansion to the west was a victory for Jefferson's vision of America as a nation of small farmers. Of course, these were not the only kind of farmers, so there were implications for slavery as the major planters began looking westward, but it would take a few years before trouble became impossible to ignore.

By 1819, the Missouri Territory had enough Americans living in it to qualify for statehood. As Congress took up the question, things got complicated. James Tallmadge was a one-term member of the House of Representatives, and he was a Democratic-Republican, the party of Jefferson, Madison, and Monroe. Tallmadge believed it was his duty as a lawmaker and a Christian to oppose slavery, so he did. Tallmadge called for adding an amendment to the Missouri statehood bill that would slowly eliminate slavery there.[66] This was the method for eradicating slavery that had already proved successful in Pennsylvania and other states.

This launched another spirited and stormy debate. Thomas Jefferson went from talking about the benefits of the death of slavery to

---

[64] Carter's story is told in Andrew Levy's *The First Emancipator: Slavery, Religion, and the Quiet Resolution of Robert Carter* (New York: Random House, 2005).
[65] Ellis (2000), 96-118.
[66] It called for no new slaves to be allowed into Missouri and for the children born of slaves already in Missouri to be freed at a certain future point.

advocating its survival in Missouri and beyond. This was an easy pivot for Jefferson, who had already written in his *Notes on the State of Virginia* how well suited Africans were for slavery, but that is an account best left for the chapter on the third president later in the book.

The Missouri debate had many facets: political balance in the Senate, economic vitality in the South, partisan political games (Jefferson claimed this despite the fact that Tallmadge was one of his own), and legal obligations based on the treaty terms of the Louisiana Purchase. In the end the forces of compromise and nationalism won out. Missouri entered the Union as a slave state, and Maine separated from Massachusetts and became a free state, so balance was maintained in the Senate and a broader agreement was made to open the door for the admission of more states in the West.

By 1820, slaves had experienced another population surge, going from a little under 700,000 in 1790 to over 1.5 million. Rather than over saturating the market, the monetary value of an average field hand had increased significantly. Cotton had overtaken tobacco as the most lucrative cash crop of the South, and cotton was much more labor intensive. There was money to be made from the labor of slaves, and the possibility of selling slaves to new plantations in the ever-expanding West was a cause worth arguing for in the minds of many southerners who previously had not wanted to speak out on this awkward topic.[67]

Thomas Jefferson, among others, suggested that allowing the South to sell its surplus slaves out West would reduce their numbers in the South, making the institution easier to eradicate there. Opponents pointed out that creating a bigger market for slaves would drive their value up, thus making it more likely that an increase of slaves would be encouraged.[68]

The Missouri debate greatly damaged civility in Congress. Moving forward, northerners were skeptical regarding southern claims of discomfort over slavery. But southerners questioned northern motives, too. Denunciations of slavery by the North were seen as

---

[67]Robert Pierce Forbes, *The Missouri Compromise and its Aftermath* (Chapel Hill: University of North Carolina Press, 2007), Kindle. L 755-762.
[68] Ibid, L 971-978.

political theatrics. Both sides continued to invoke Christianity. The South talked about their support for missions and Bible distributions, the North called slavery a sin, and they just kept talking past each other.[69]

Before the 1830s, the only group working seriously on a national level towards a future without slavery was the American Colonization Society, which sought to send African Americans to Africa.[70] It should be understood that for the most part when this took place the ex-slaves were not sent *back* to Africa. Most of the slaves had been born in the United States at this point. Even for those who were first generation slaves, they were not from the area where the new colony was planted: Liberia.

It should also be noted that the people behind the ACS were driven to a degree by racism—by not wanting to share the country with people of African descent—but there was more to it than that. Slavery was seen as the worst evil; this alternate plan would be a better thing for master and slave. Also, it bears mentioning that, as Robert Pierce Forbes points out, "They simply had no model available to them of a successful multicultural republic."[71]

There were connections between religion and the colonization project. Smith Thompson, who supported the American Colonization Society, was also the Vice President of the American Bible Society. And missionaries helped with the startup of the colonies in Liberia, even as malaria and other diseases were raging there.[72]

Ultimately, the plan to free slaves and send them to Africa failed for several reasons. It was too expensive, many African Americans were leery of getting on ships to go to faraway lands—who knew what was *really* waiting for them on the other side? It did not work out too well for their people the last time they crossed the ocean—and many owners were simply not willing to give up what they had.

A slave and preacher named Nat Turner led a revolt in Virginia in 1831, which only ended after the deaths of over fifty whites. Many in

---

[69] Forbes, L 935, 964-971.
[70] Ibid., L 578.
[71] Forbes, L 585-592.
[72] Ibid., L 538, 635-642.

the South stopped entertaining the idea of somehow freeing their slaves after this. For those abolitionists who were slow to get the message, the threat and then reality of mob violence soon made it clear that abolitionists needed to move to the North or just shut up. Suspicions even arose against the American Colonization Society.[73]

As people on both sides of the slavery issue fought for their positions, they made faith-based arguments. Both slavery and faith held prominent places in the cultural landscape. These topics were simply too big for the presidents to ignore. How did the presidents deal with these matters? That is a key question for the next six chapters.

---

[73] Ahlstrom, Volume 2, 98.

CHAPTER 3

GEORGE WASHINGTON

John Adams had a rare gift for seeing the worst in people. Nevertheless, in a letter to his wife, he described George Washington as "modest and virtuous…amiable, generous, and brave."[74] When Abigail Adams finally saw Washington in person, she wrote to her husband, "You had prepared me to entertain a favorable opinion of him, but I thought the one half was not told me."[75] Modern translation: Washington was twice as awesome as Mrs. Adams thought he would be.

Who was George Washington? Was he a Christian champion of liberty or a Deist slave owner? Was he a Deist champion of liberty or a Christian who owned slaves? Might he somehow have been a little bit of all of the above? What can one learn definitively about Washington regarding faith, race, and leadership? In this chapter more attention will be paid to religion because there is so much interesting material and commentary available today on Washington's faith.

A reality that complicates our understanding of George Washington is his famously reserved nature. He did not talk much about himself or his feelings.[76] He once communicated to his officers

---

[74] Frank Shuffelton, Editor, *The Letters of John and Abigail Adams* (New York: Penguin Books, 2004), 63.
[75] Joseph J. Ellis, *First Family* (New York: Vintage Books, 2011), 46.

during the Revolution that they should "be easy...but not too familiar" with their men.[77] Washington was talking about military leadership in this context, but he tended to be formal and restrained in other leadership roles, too, and as a politically active, rich Virginia plantation owner, there were few occasions when Washington was not acting in a position of leadership. When Washington concluded his formal oath of office by adding the phrase "so help me God" then leaned forward and kissed the Bible at his inauguration,[78] it was such a fascinating gesture at least partially because he was such a reserved man. And yet, as a learned colleague pointed out, kissing the Bible is not the same as reading it,[79] so how much does even that gesture tell us?

As a child, Washington was educated at an Anglican school. James Monroe's biographer Harlow Giles Unger describes such academies as being run by Anglican clergymen who taught their pupils about the Bible along with math, history, Latin and French.[80]

Despite the fact that they were raised as churchgoers and educated by the clergy, historian David L. Holmes was convinced that all of the early Virginian presidents believed in some form of Deism.[81] Supporting evidence for this position, as it relates to George Washington, can be found in the writings of Bishop William White, who was a contemporary of Washington's and knew the first president in Philadelphia and New York. The bishop said, "I do not believe that any degree of recollection will bring to my mind any fact that would prove General Washington to have been a believer in the Christian revelation."[82]

---

[76] Joseph J. Ellis, *His Excellency: George Washington* (New York: Alfred A. Knopf, 2004), 37-39.

[77] David McCullough, *1776* (New York: Simon & Schuster, 2005), 43.

[78] Lynne Cheney, *James Madison* (New York: Viking, 2014), 187.

[79] Thank you, Chad Gregory.

[80] Harlow Giles Unger, *The Last Founding Father* (Philadelphia: Da Capo Press, 2009), 12.

[81] David L. Holmes, *The Faiths of the Founding Fathers* (New York: Oxford University Press, 2006), 36.

[82] Jon Meacham, *American Gospel* New York: Random House, 2007), 78.

Curiously, though, Washington the would-be Deist was quite active in his home church. For one thing, he served as a vestryman for over twenty years. The vestry had immense power in Anglican churches, even determining where congregants would sit, with the goal of "preserving order, decency, peace, and harmony," as recorded by a church upon its foundation in 1736.[83] The vestry collected church taxes and paid the local parson's salary.[84] Though this was actually a political office, those who held the position did more than just wield power over their fellow citizens. "The vestry did things like look after the poor and purchase the elements for Communion," according to Mary Thompson, an expert on religion in the life of George Washington.[85] When the future president took the oath to join the vestry in 1762, he had to affirm the deity of Christ, His resurrection from the dead, and His ascension into Heaven.[86] Washington also served multiple terms as churchwarden, which oversaw the care of widows and orphans, and had its own Christian oath. Because of the size of Mount Vernon, Washington also found himself inside the boundary of a neighboring church parish, so he rented a pew and joined the vestry there, too, once again affirming in oath his belief in the deity of Christ and His redemptive work in salvation.[87]

Additionally, Washington was the godfather of at least eight children over the course of his life. The religious service for this required Washington to display an orthodox Christian faith.[88] It seems a little hard to believe that the honor-bound Washington would have been so involved in these roles in his church if he did not embrace the belief system.

One could discount the vestry evidence by arguing that Thomas Jefferson was also elected as a vestryman, and he clearly did not

---

[83] John K. Nelson, *A Blessed Company* (Chapel Hill: University of North Carolina Press, 2002), L 3722.

[84] Mary V. Thompson, *In the Hands of a Good Providence* (Charlottesville: University of Virginia Press, 2008). 40.

[85] Mary Thompson, interview with author, March 26, 2015.

[86] Peter A. Lillback with Jerry Newcombe *George Washington's Sacred Fire* (Bryn Mawr, PA: Providence Forum Press, 2006), 91.

[87] Ron Chernow, *Washington* (New York: Penguin Books, 2011), 130.

[88] Lillback with Newcombe, 106.

believe in the deity of Christ. But Jefferson was only chosen to serve in the vestry; he did not actually do the job.[89] Also, Jefferson refused to be a godparent because he did not agree with the religious oath required of a godparent in the Anglican Church.[90] There is a pretty clear distinction between Washington and Jefferson here.

While fighting in the French and Indian War, Washington wrote to his brother on July 18, 1755, "I now exist and appear in the land of the living by the miraculous care of Providence that protected me beyond all human expectation. I had four bullets through my coat, and two horses shot under me, and yet I escaped." Almost thirty years later, Washington spent time editing his personal papers. When he found this letter circa 1784-1785, he added "But by the all-powerful dispensations of Providence, I have been protected beyond all human probability and expectation."[91] This certainly seems like the language of a man who believes that God intervenes in the affairs of people, not a Deist who thinks that the Almighty stays out of humanity's business.

Washington ordered his men to attend a worship service in the French and Indian War on September 26, 1756. He also sent at least four letters to the authorities in Virginia requesting that a chaplain be provided for the Virginia troops. At least part of his concern, though, centered on the deportment of his forces. He complained that without a chaplain to encourage them to do better, the soldiers were drinking too much.[92] Washington was no prohibitionist, but the man appreciated appropriate behavior. Of course, a desire for disciplined troops is not truly evidence of faith.

Was Washington a man of prayer? In his first Inaugural Address on April 30, 1789, he spoke of his "fervent supplications to that Almighty Being who rules over the universe." In the same brief

---

[89] Bishop William Meade, *Old Churches, Ministers, and Families of Virginia.*(Philadelphia: J.B. Lippincott and Co., 2011), Kindle, Location 835-841.
[90] Lillback with Newcombe, 515-516.
[91] Editor John C. Fitzpatrick, *The Writings of George Washington from the Original Manuscript Sources*, Volume 1 (Washington DC: US Government Printing Office, 1931), 152.
[92] Ibid., 466, 470, 473, 498, and 505.

address, Washington paid "homage to the Great Author of every public and private good" and made other references to God.[93]

Evangelical biographer Robert W. Pelton casts Washington as a devout man based on the famous painting of the general kneeling in the snow and praying, as witnessed by a Quaker who had been opposed to the Revolutionary War until he spied the Continental Army's Commander in Chief beseeching God.[94] But this story has been discredited given that the Quaker in question did not live on the land where he allegedly saw Washington, and Washington typically did not kneel when he prayed.[95] Part of what makes the study of Washington so complicated is that almost every argument has a counter argument. It is possible for a man to visit a piece of property before buying it, and just because Washington usually stood in prayer does not mean he never made an exception.

Tim LaHaye believes that if one read the prayers of George Washington objectively, it would indicate clearly that "were George Washington living today, he would freely identify with the Bible-believing branch of evangelical Christianity." LaHaye points to writings in Washington's personal prayer book,[96] some samples of which will be seen below.

One is left to wonder, though, if LaHaye has overreached here. Washington was loyal to the denomination in which he grew up, and he was an extremely reserved man. If he were born today into a not-so-evangelical congregation, there is little to suggest he would switch to a different church. Of course, if he were born into the world of contemporary American narcissism, complete with people sharing their innermost thoughts on social media, perhaps he would be less reserved anyway.

---

[93] John Gabriel Hunt, *The Inaugural Address of the Presidents* (New York: Gramercy Books, 2003), 4-7.

[94] Robert W. Pelton, *George Washington's Prophetic Vision* (West Conshohocken, PA: Infinity Publishing Company, 2007), 37.

[95] Holmes, 70. That Washington did not kneel in prayer was also affirmed by the historian Ron Chernow, p. 131.

[96] Tim LaHaye, *Faith of the Founding Fathers* (Master Books, 1994, 1893-1942, Kindle.

Regardless of Washington's inclusive and generic religious language in public, the man might have used more explicitly Christian language privately. His personal prayer book contains references like "O most glorious God, in Jesus Christ my merciful and loving Father, I acknowledge and confess my guilt," and "into Thy hands I commend myself, both soul and body, in the name of Thy Son, Jesus Christ." There are other examples,[97] and these personal writings possibly tell the reader much about this private man. Perhaps he drifted from these views later in life. He was only about twenty years old when he created this journal, and such overt language is not in evidence later, but what would have caused such a drift? He was a private man who lived a public life—where is the evidence of an event that caused a theological shift? There does not have to be a public event to cause a change of perspective, but it would help those who believe Washington was religiously indifferent to make their case.

The problem with the prayer book evidence, cited by LaHaye among others, is that some historians believe it is not in Washington's handwriting. Likewise, several of Washington's fellow officers say that he was a man who spent regular time in private prayer, but some historians discount their reports because they were passed along orally before later being written down by others.[98] Of course the reality is that much of history was passed down orally before being recorded, so that really should not be an issue here. Regarding the prayer book specifically though, Mary Thompson's theory is that it was actually written by another family member and authorship was mistakenly attributed to Washington later.[99]

Guests in Washington's home, Mount Vernon, recall him getting up early, some said by five AM, and saying his prayers. Others said he would say grace before meals unless a clergyman was present in which case Washington would defer. He had the same practice when not at home—giving the blessing over the meal unless a minister was there.[100]

---

[97] William J. Federer, *America's God and Country: Encyclopedia of Quotations* (St. Louis: Amerisearch, 2000), 658-659.
[98] Thompson, 92.
[99] Thompson interview.

The bottom line is that Washington prayed more than some secularists want to admit, but his prayers were probably not as evangelically-tinged as some Christians want to believe.

Author Peter A. Lillback makes a point that is rather startling in its simplicity. "Washington never declared himself to be a Deist, and he did declare himself to be a Christian."[101] That said, other Founders also claimed to be Christians, yet their theology told another story.

The debate over Washington's faith started early. James Madison worked as a political ally of Washington for several years. In fact Madison was so trusted by Washington that Madison played a major part in writing Washington's Farewell Address.[102] In 1830 Madison wrote that Washington probably never questioned the established religion. "But he took these things as he found them existing, and was constant in his observations of worship according to the received forms of the Episcopal [Anglican] church in which he was raised."[103] The influential Chief Justice of the Supreme Court John Marshall was also a man who knew Washington well. Marshall writes, "Without making ostentatious professions of religion, he was a sincere believer in the Christian faith, and a truly devout man."[104] However Thomas Jefferson, too, knew Washington, serving in his administration as the first secretary of state. Jefferson once said of Washington that he "has [ministers] constantly about him because he thinks it right to keep up appearances but is an unbeliever."[105] Were these fellow Virginians giving dispassionate perceptions of Washington, or were they, like so

---

[100] Thompson, 94-97.

[101] Lillback with Newcombe, 143.

[102] Actually, Madison wrote a first draft when Washington considering retiring in 1792, and this document served as starting point for Washington's actual Farewell Address that was given at the end of Washington's second term in 1796. Alexander Hamilton and of course Washington himself also played a major role in the Address. Stuart Leibiger, *Founding Friendship* (Charlottesville: University of Virginia Press, 2001), 161, 209.

[103] Holmes, 70-71.

[104] John Marshall, *The Life of George Washington* (Edwards Publishing House, 2011), L. 21403-21405.

[105] Thompson, 1.

many people, guilty of seeing what they wanted to see? In Jefferson's case, was he trying to subtly malign a man whom Jefferson began to see as a political enemy, or was Jefferson guilty of projecting what would have been his own motives for such behavior on an innocent man? Ron Chernow, who wrote a Pulitzer Prize winning biography of Washington, makes an interesting point about Jefferson's overall take on the first president's faith. Jefferson had also told a story about Washington refusing to agree to the request of some religious leaders to openly declare his beliefs. Apparently, Jefferson heard this second hand and got the facts wrong according to Dr. Ashbel Green, who had shared the account with Jefferson in the first place.[106]

Eleanor Parke Custis Lewis, the adopted granddaughter of the first president, writes, "I should have thought it the greatest heresy to doubt (Washington's) firm belief in Christianity. His life, his writings, prove that he was a Christian."[107]

Episcopal Bishop William Meade, who in the 1850s wrote a history of the leading families of Virginia, acknowledges that there were some who had a "philosophic belief in Providence which is little better than atheism," but he argued that Washington's faith was different. Among other things, Meade cites the aforementioned letter Washington wrote to his brother during the French and Indian War when Washington said, "By the all-powerful dispensations of Providence, I have been protected beyond all human probability or expectation."[108]

Meade believed that Washington was a Christian, but one might argue that as an Episcopal bishop, Meade had an incentive to talk up the faith of famous Americans. Yet Meade did not believe that Jefferson was a Christian.

During the Revolutionary War, officers and enlisted men who were not on duty had mandatory attendance required for religious services, mandated by Washington. Even the irreligious in Washington's day saw the value of religion in maintaining order among

---

[106] Chernow, 130.
[107] Pelton, 9, 12. The Lewis quotation is also found in Lillback with Newcombe, 721.
[108] Meade, L 4596-4600.

the masses, but Washington's support of religion seems to be greater than that. When a chaplain was not available, Washington would read the service himself. David L. Holmes writes, "By the standards of the eighteenth century, Washington was religiously active."[109] A reasonable person might argue that leading worship services might qualify for a stronger concession than merely "religiously active."

Once during the Revolutionary War when Washington's men got a little out of line, he said to them, "The general hopes and trusts that every officer and man will endeavor so to live and act as becomes a Christian soldier." Also, after the Americans' pivotal victory at Saratoga, Washington ordered his chaplains to come up with an appropriate discourse for the benefit of the troops.[110] While such examples do not prove that he was an evangelical, it is easy to argue that Washington was comfortable with faith.

It was during his presidency that the First Amendment was passed with his approval, thus guaranteeing freedom of religion. Stuart Leibiger writes, "In answering Jews, Catholics, Quakers, and other denominations, Washington promoted religious freedom by publicly acknowledging each sect's Revolutionary contributions and by welcoming their immigrant brethren to America."[111] Washington believed, as he once said, "It is the duty of all nations to acknowledge the providence of Almighty God, to obey His will, to be grateful for his benefits, and humbly to implore his protection and favor."[112]

Skeptics regarding Washington's faith can cite Washington's pastor during the first presidency. This pastor says, "I never heard anything from him that could manifest his opinions on the subject of religion." On the other hand, Washington's step-granddaughter Eleanor Lewis says, "I never heard him relate a single act of his life during the war."[113] The modern reader knows that Washington was pretty involved in the latter, and had strong feelings on the subject, so one should not necessarily assume Washington's indifference to the former.

---

[109] Holmes, 59.
[110] Jon Meacham, *American Gospel* (New York: Random House, 2007) 77.
[111] Leibiger, 121.
[112] LaHaye, 1823.
[113] Thompson, 8-9.

Joseph J. Ellis describes Washington as "a lukewarm Episcopalian," noting that "he never took Communion, tended to talk about 'Providence' or 'Destiny' rather than God, and—was this a statement?—preferred to stand rather than kneel when praying."[114] However, Washington's granddaughter Eleanor Lewis argues that most people did not kneel in this time period. Martha Washington still did, but she was the exception.[115]

The Communion charge, though, is harder to dismiss. At a minimum, for long stretches of time Washington did not participate in the Communion ritual performed in his church. Would that qualify him as irreligious? We do know that Washington provided wine for his church's Communion services,[116] but how does one explain his lack of personal participation in the rite?

Interestingly, according to Rhys Isaac, only a few elderly people tended to participate in Communion in Anglican Churches in Virginia during the eighteenth century.[117] Nevertheless, a few historians have offered up theories for why George Washington, specifically, chose not to be involved. Alf J. Mapp, Jr. wonders if Washington felt inadequate to participate because of his reliance on the King James Bible. Mapp points out that this translation urges the believer to not partake of Communion "unworthily," lest he/she risk damnation. Could a man with Washington's high standards consider himself worthy? Mapp suggests maybe not.[118] Ron Chernow suggests that the very reserved and private Washington would have simply been uncomfortable with such an open display of religiosity.[119] Bishop William Meade, laments that there were many in the United States and Britain who got caught up in a belief that continuing to participate in the Lord's Supper was simply not that important.[120] David L. Holmes writes, "Except during

---

[114] Ellis, *Washington*, 45.
[115] Thompson interview; Lillback with Newcombe, 721.
[116] Thompson, 77.
[117] Rhys Isaac, *The Transformation of Virginia* (Chapel Hill: UNC Press, 1982), 120.
[118] Alf J. Mapp, Jr., *The Faiths of our Founders* (New York: Fall River Press, 2006), 78-79.
[119] Chernow, 131-132.
[120] Meade, L. 9056.

Easter, the percentage of churchgoers who remained for the Communion in the eighteenth century was generally low, although some Anglican parishes were exceptions."[121]

Granddaughter Eleanor Lewis claims that her mother said George Washington frequently took Communion with his wife Martha before the Revolutionary War. A pastor also claimed that Washington participated in this sacrament during the Revolution at a Presbyterian Church in New Jersey. Mary Thompson, who wrote a book on Washington's religious views, suggests that his reason for not taking Communion and for resigning as a vestryman might be the same. Washington could not countenance the continued observance of oaths to the head of a church who was also the British king against whom Washington had just fought a war.[122] After the Episcopal Church was established in America, it was not too long before Washington was tied up in the Constitutional Convention and the presidency, which might have explained why he did not resume his duties as a vestryman, though it would not explain an absence at the Communion table. But maybe he was not absent for long. Several people claimed over the years that they or relatives had seen Washington taking Communion on various occasions.[123]

A trip to Washington's tomb at Mt. Vernon reveals the inscription from John 11:25-26, which says, "I am the Resurrection and the life." Did Washington pick out his own verses? They would certainly say something about his beliefs. According to a Mt. Vernon tour guide, some historians believe he did. But since Mr. and Mrs. Washingtons' bodies were moved from their original crypt to a different location in a new crypt, it is possible that another family member picked out the Scripture.[124] Peter A. Lillback believes that Washington's heirs picked the text.[125] Given that Lillback argues in his book that Washington was a Christian, it is interesting that Lillback

---

[121] Holmes, 63.
[122] Thompson, 77-80.
[123] Lillback with Newcombe, 411-417, 453, 513-514.
[124] I was there June 21, 2014.
[125] Lillback with Newcombe, 265.

concedes this point. One might conclude that this gives credibility to this historian's overall judgement.

Washington's personal library contained several books critical of Deism. One book it did not contain was Thomas Paine's *Age of Reason* with its hostility towards Christianity.[126] Should something be read into that?

As stated above, there are many who believe that Washington was not orthodox in his beliefs, but there can be little debate that religion played a large role in his life. He saw how religion could unify an army, and he believed he personally experienced the benefits of serving a benevolent and active God. Finally, he believed that religion encouraged good citizenship. Washington was a promoter of faith. Washington did not share his views on the finer points of theology, but he was comfortable being a leader in his church, and when the situation called for it during the war, leading worship out in the field. The evidence seems to lean in favor of Washington being a Christian.

One is left to wonder, therefore, what it meant when, late in George Washington's second term as president, he had one of his diplomats produce a document that read in part "the government of the United States of America is not in any sense founded on the Christian religion?" What did it mean when the Senate approved the treaty with the pirates of North Africa, and the new president, John Adams, signed it?[127] What did that say about Washington's religion, and what did it say about him as a leader?

A reasonable answer to this would be that one did not have to be a member of a government-endorsed church to hold office in the USA, the way one did in Britain or Spain. Since the American government was not officially representing a specific non-Muslim religion, there was not a natural need for tension between the United States and Muslim pirates attacking American shipping off the coast of North Africa.

---

[126] Lillback with Newcombe , 514.

[127] The context of the language was a conflict with Muslim pirates off the Barbary Coast of North Africa, but it is striking rhetoric nevertheless. Jon Meacham, *American Gospel* (New York: Random House, 2007), 103.

This points to Washington's pragmatism as a leader, which will be dealt with in greater detail below. He was not the philosophical idealist that Jefferson was. Washington did not write inspiring words about freedom; he went and fought for it.[128] In Washington's "Address to the Cherokee Nation," written in 1796, the last full year of his presidency, he encouraged the Cherokee to assimilate into the mainstream culture. Washington thought they should abandon their former ways and take up farming, not because it was fair, but because it was the best way for their people to thrive as they moved forward.[129]

We learn something about Washington's faith and his character after he won the Revolutionary War and appeared before the Continental Congress. Unlike Caesar or Napoleon, Washington did not use his success and fame to claim power for himself. He said to the Congress, "I consider it an indispensable duty to close this last solemn act of my official life by commending the interests of our dearest country to the protection of Almighty God."[130] There was no playing to the crowd here—Washington was leaving. There was no Constitution outlining an office of the presidency. Washington was telling the governing body of the land that he was retiring, so he hardly seemed to be lobbying for a position in it, unless he was playing hard to get.

One attack on Washington's character and reputation as a leader that has been launched in recent years is that he was a slave owner. The argument goes that if he was such a great man, he should have freed his slaves, or better yet, fought to end slavery in the new nation altogether. How could a man fight a war for freedom and then deny freedom to other human beings living on his property?

Washington's history with slavery started out pretty unremarkably. He was a slave owner in a slave owning culture. Rather than wishing for their freedom, he suffered the frustrations common to owners, like trying to track down runaways.[131]

---

[128] This is not a criticism of Jefferson here. Successful revolutions usually require both inspiring words and inspiring actions.

[129] Rhodehamel, 956-960.

[130] Harlow Giles Unger, *The Last Founding Father* (Philadelphia: Da Capo Press, 2010), 50.

Washington began to see things differently over time. He told a cousin during the Revolutionary War that he wanted to get out of the practice of being a slave owner.[132] But Washington faced the logistical issue that every slave owner had—despite apparent wealth relative to his neighbors, he struggled to pay his bills. He found it difficult to imagine how to survive if he suddenly had to compensate his workers.

If that was not enough, there was another complication for Washington. He had three hundred and eighteen slaves living on his property, but he only owned one hundred and twenty-three of them. The rest were slaves that his wife Martha brought into the marriage. They were part of the inheritance for her and her late husband's children and their extended family. Washington could have freed his slaves, but not hers. Furthermore, the two groups had intermarried over the years, and freed slaves were expected to leave the area. The children of such unions would lose a parent if one were freed, and elderly slaves could not be released—owners were supposed to care for them as a matter of state law. Thus, there was little he felt he could do to free most of his slaves. George Washington stipulated that his slaves would be freed after he and Martha were deceased because at that point they would be divided anyway, so the transition would be easier. He further stipulated that his assets would be sold to aid the slaves in their transition to freedom. Historian Mary Thompson wonders if it was Washington's guilt over slavery that caused him to refuse Communion.[133]

What kind of leader was Washington? According to one of his generals, Nathanael Greene, he was "universally admired."[134]

As a leader, part of what helped Washington fill the role was simply his imposing physical presence. In addition to being an almost legendary horseman, Washington had a reputation for throwing things—stones, iron bars, whatever the young men happened to be throwing that day—farther than any of his peers.[135] Men were inspired

---

[131] John Rhodehamel, editor, *Washington: Writings* (New York: The Library of America, 1997), 102-103.

[132] Thompson, 84.

[133] Ibid., 88-90.

[134] McCullough (2005), 20.

to follow him partially from the sheer physicality of the tall, strong man.

According to Ralph Ketcham, Washington "had little taste for political theory," but the first president had a "deep self-consciousness of his unique role." Thus Washington fit the description made by Lord Bolingbroke, an Enlightenment contemporary of Voltaire, of the patriot king.[136] For Washington and his five successors, this was their goal: to put leadership and loyalty to their country before personal popularity or political party.

Unfortunately for Washington, though, political parties quickly developed. In Washington's small Cabinet, both sides were represented. The Federalist Party was guided by Alexander Hamilton, the first secretary of the treasury and a former military aide of Washington's during the war. The Democratic-Republicans were openly led by James Madison from his position in the House of Representatives. But Madison was collaborating with Thomas Jefferson, Washington's secretary of state. As Ketcham points out, it was difficult for Washington to carve out a middle path between Hamilton and Jefferson, and it really bothered the first president when he was accused of favoring one side.[137] Given Washington's structured, disciplined, and martial background—and his shared experience with the loyal Hamilton in the army—it is not shocking that Washington tended to favor Hamilton's vision of a strong federal government, but Washington was determined to not be a Federalist. He wanted to be everyone's president, not just the leader of one side of the debate.

An example of Washington's desire to be above politics can be seen in how he walked away from the presidency. He considered retiring after his first four-year term, and he was so serious about this that he had James Madison write a farewell address. When he stayed on for another four years, he had Hamilton take a stab at it. The final product communicated Washington's views, but it also reflected Madison's work with Hamilton's input included, too. Washington

---

[135] McCullough (2005), 48.
[136] Ralph Ketcham, *Presidents above Party* (Chapel Hill: University of North Carolina Press, 1984), 57-61, 89
[137] Ibid., 92.

relied on a leading Democratic-Republican and a leading Federalist for this important task.

Henry Lee, who had served with Washington during the Revolutionary War, eulogized the man as "first in war, first in peace, first in the hearts of his countrymen." He was a man of faith and good character, but could he have done more to combat slavery? Technically, the answer is yes, but it should be noted that he did do more than most of his peers.
He could have spoken out forcefully, and his stature was such that it might have moved the needle some. It also would have threatened Washington's chances to be president. If Washington had not been there to hold the country together, the Constitution might have foundered, if it would have even been accepted in the first place, and slavery would have continued anyway. Washington freed more slaves under his direct control than any of the other presidents in this study, but a few of his immediate successors had a bigger impact on the issue overall. As a leader Washington was be-loved by those who knew him, reserved, and pragmatic without being cynical. He inspired people.

CHAPTER 4

#2 JOHN ADAMS

John Adams wanted to be above the political parties, just as Washington was before him. But Adams had even less success because of, as Ralph Ketcham points out, Adams' "temperament, reputation, and circumstances."[138] This is a polite way of saying Adams could be combustible and irritating, and he had not earned the respect that comes with successfully leading a ragtag army against the world's number one superpower.

How do you follow greatness? For Adams this was not just a philosophical consideration. As the successor to Washington, Adams had to deal with the shadow of the tall Virginian, and the presidency was not the only arena in which Adams came up second. The Massachusetts native was quite the diplomat, representing American interests in Britain and France, but he never enjoyed the esteem of the remarkable Ben Franklin. Adams was respected enough to be on the committee that created the Declaration of Independence, but Thomas Jefferson gets most of the credit for writing it. Whatever the talented and brilliant Adams committed himself to, wherever he tried to leave his mark and make a difference, there was always someone a little bit greater who was there to overshadow him.

Historian Joseph J. Ellis points out the amazing irony of Adams' life: The man was consumed with a desire for personal

---

[138] Ralph Ketcham, *President above Party* (Chapel Hill: University of North Carolina Press, 1984), 95.

greatness, but perhaps his most significant contributions to American history were his recommendations for other men to serve in ways that ultimately overshadowed him. It was Adams who suggested to the Continental Congress that George Washington become the commander of the Continental Army during the Revolutionary War. Adams also thought that Jefferson should pen the Declaration of Independence. Finally, Adams was the man who suggested that John Marshall be installed as Chief Justice of the Supreme Court. Marshall is obviously the least famous of these figures today, but Ellis says Marshall was "without much question the most towering and influential chief justice in American history.[139]

In short: Adams was no Washington, Jefferson, Franklin, or Marshall. So, who was John Adams? What can one make of his views on religion, race, and leadership?

Adams was baptized in the Congregationalist Church—the church of the Puritans, and he was the son of such a committed lay leader, that Adams' father was called "Deacon John."[140] Yet despite John Adams' orthodox upbringing, author Steven Waldman characterized our second President as "religiously complex." John Adams was a deeply religious man, but he hated what he perceived as "a spirit of dogmatism and bigotry in clergy and laity."[141] He disliked religious leaders who seemed more interested in holding on to their power than in the pursuit of honest intellectual inquiry.

The above sentiments would not be foreign to many evangelicals today, but Adams had some views that would definitely fall outside of traditional evangelical thought. He generally disliked Calvinists and Catholics—positions which would garner mixed reviews from evangelicals today. But on some things he was totally across the line. He thought the concept of the Trinity was illogical, and the doctrine of salvation by faith alone was bad because it could "discourage the practice of virtue."[142]

---

[139] Joseph J. Ellis, *First Family* (New York: Vintage Books, 2011), 46-47, 211. Marshall was significant for pushing through the Supreme Court the decision that gave the Court the power of judicial review.

[140] David McCullough, *John Adams* (New York: Touchstone Book, 2002), 29.

[141] Steven Waldman, *Founding Faith* (New York: Random House, 2008) 32, 34.

Adams' church would eventually become Unitarian. While Unitarians today tend to take a very loose standard when it comes to what their followers believe, back then they thought of themselves as Christians. Adams was so impressed by Christianity he once said, "Neither savage nor civilized man, without a revelation, could ever have discovered or invented it." And like Washington, Adams believed that Christianity was necessary for curbing the sinful impulses of humanity.[143] As Adams put it in a letter to Thomas Jefferson, "Without religion this world would be something not fit to be mentioned in polite company, I mean Hell."[144] It was certainly easier to govern people who were already given an incentive by virtue of their faith to act decently to one another.

According to acclaimed historian David McCullough, "Adams was both a devout Christian and an independent thinker, and he saw no conflict in that."[145] Adams liked the writings of Bolingbroke on political leadership, but Adams was critical of the man's rejection of orthodox Christianity in favor of Deism.[146]

Interestingly, historian Joseph J. Ellis says that Adams was not like the typical Puritan, despite the man's Massachusetts roots. Rather than asking "Am I saved?" Adams was more interested in the question "What is my destiny?" Thus, it is not surprising that Adams resisted the wishes of his father, and the career path of his father-in-law, and became a lawyer instead of a minister.[147]

Adams' public commitment to faith was more than just an affectation meant to win votes with the religious crowd; it was central to who he was. In just one letter to Abigail, dated July 1, 1774, John Adams referenced God three times. Adams wrote of keeping a clear conscience before God, he thanked God for His generosity in the personal gifts He gave to Adams, and he prayed for Abigail's health.[148]

---

[142] Waldman, 35.
[143] Ibid., 36-37.
[144] Jon Meacham, *American Gospel* (New York: Random House, 2007), 28.
[145] McCullough, 19.
[146] Ketcham, 100.
[147] Ellis, 9-10.
[148] Frank Shuffelton, Editor, *The Letters of John and Abigail Adams* (New York:

Despite Adams' disbelief in significant traditional Christian tenets about the nature of Christ—specifically the deity of Christ and the atoning work of His death on the Cross—Adams sometimes displayed a high regard for Scripture. When Thomas Paine's *Common Sense* was published, Adams was not impressed. Adams found Paine's comments regarding the Old Testament to be "ridiculous," and Adams was so exercised on the subject that he confronted Paine about it.[149]

On a similar note, when a suggestion was made in the Continental Congress for a fast day, Thomas Jefferson—in a rare display of honesty regarding an unpopular opinion on his part—argued against it. In the process, Jefferson cast Christianity in an unfavorable light, and Adams strongly opposed him.[150]

Of course, confronting men over the faith does not in and of itself make one a Christian, especially in the case of Adams, who often relished a spirited clash of ideas.[151]

Adams had a healthy respect for the benefits of the faith. Historian Charles N. Edel notes that "It was important to John and Abigail Adams that their children learned...the personal morality of Christianity." The Adams believed there was more to a person's character than just personal morality for civic duty was important also, but personal morality was critically important, and Christianity provided a useful guide.[152]

The future second president had at least a degree of an ecumenical outlook. Despite his low opinion of Catholicism, as a member of the Continental Congress, he attended his first Catholic Mass and raved about the wonder of it in a letter to his wife.[153] That said, he was concerned about how the mysticism of it held the people

---

Penguin Books, 2004), 8.

[149] *Adams*, 108-109.

[150] McCullough, 113.

[151] King Henry VIII of England was formally designated as a "Defender of the Faith" by a Pope, but the six-time husband and philanderer is hardly held up as an example of what it means to be a Christian.

[152] Charles N. Edel, *Nation Builder* (Cambridge, MA: Harvard University Press, 2014) 23.

[153] Ellis, 33-34.

under its spell, and he was rather appalled at the Crucifix with the image of Jesus covered with wounds and blood.[154]

Actually, Adams attended several different kinds of churches in those days, going to services two or three times each Sunday.[155]

After the fighting in the Revolutionary War had already started, but before independence was declared, Adams wrote approvingly of the widespread participation in a fast in which he took part.[156]

"Our Constitution was made for a religious people. It is wholly inadequate to the government of any other," said Adams in a letter to some soldiers in October 1798.

Adams' last presidential address was made to Congress, which had assembled in DC after the move of the government headquarters from Philadelphia to our current national capital. Adams said, "It would be unbecoming...to assemble for this first time in this solemn temple without looking up to the Supreme Ruler of the universe and imploring His blessing."[157]

Adams said in an 1816 letter to Jefferson that Adams agreed with his successor that Jesus was "the most benevolent Being that ever appeared on Earth," and in the same letter Adams lamented that people and nations did not live by the Golden Rule.[158] Later in the year, Adams wrote again to Jefferson and disparaged the works of some of those who attacked the reliability of the Bible. Adams said to his friend that the two of them should write a statement on faith and until then these other, would-be experts should just be quiet and "observe the Commandments and the Sermon on the Mount."[159]

Adams returns to this theme in a letter dated November 4, 1816. He wrote to Jefferson, "The Ten Commandments and the Sermon on the Mount contain my religion."[160] Unfortunately, this leaves out the

---

[154] McCullough, 84.
[155] Ibid., 83.
[156] This was in a letter to Abigail dated July 23, 1775. Shuffelton, 83.
[157] McCullough, 554.
[158] J. Jefferson Looney, Editor, *The Papers of Thomas Jefferson,* Volume 9 (Princeton, NJ: Princeton University Press, 2012), 431-432.
[159] J. Jefferson Looney, Editor, *The Papers of Thomas Jefferson,* Volume 10 (Princeton, NJ: Princeton University Press, 2013), 424-425.
[160] Looney, Volume 10, 507-508.

central themes of Christianity: the divinity of Christ, His death and resurrection, and His payment of the price for the sins of those who believe.

A month later, Adams' theology had grown more succinct. In another letter to Jefferson, this one dated December 12, 1816, Adams said, "My moral or religious creed...for 50 or 60 years (has) been contained in four short words: be just and good."[161]

Late in life the second president still expressed himself with Puritan language. He couched future plans in expressions like, "If it is the will of Heaven."[162]

Ultimately, what was John Adams? If he could speak to the reader today from across time, he would call himself a Christian, and he would be rather noisy about it. He wouldn't just claim the label to win votes in the Bible belt. But despite his fervor, by any traditional, orthodox definition of what it means to be a Christian as defined in the Bible, John Adams would be a well-meaning heretic. Such was the personality of the man that he criticized others for questioning the Bible even though he also did not follow its theological statements.

One would think that Adams would be rated rather favorably on the slavery issue. He never owned slaves, he did not like slavery, and he wrote the Massachusetts state constitution in such a way that the Massachusetts Supreme Court ruled that slave ownership was illegal in their state.[163] Even getting this opportunity tells us something about Adams as a leader. During the Revolutionary War, 250 delegates got together to put together a state constitution. A committee of thirty was selected, then a subcommittee of three, and among the three subcommittee members the other two decided that Adams should put together the draft.[164]

Despite all of that, author Kenneth O'Reilly puts a negative spin on Adams when it comes to this issue. O'Reilly's characterization of the man makes the second president look like someone who was

---

[161] Ibid., 573.
[162] McCullough, 286.
[163] Ellis, 128.
[164] McCullough, 220.

personally opposed to slavery, but was too weak-willed or politically craven to really stand against it.[165]

The above characterization is unfair. Despite having friends who owned slaves, Adams wrote that the institution was incompatible with reason, justice, and humanity."[166] Despite that, as we shall see below, Adams liked taking unpopular stands, so whatever his flaws, he was decidedly not weak-willed.

Abigail Adams grew up in a family that owned two slaves, but she was not of the opinion that African Americans were mentally inferior. Her husband also must have been free from that bias based on a domestic decision John and Abigail made. In 1784, Abigail went overseas to join her husband in Britain. While they were there, they left Phoebe Abdee, a former slave, in charge of their home [167]

Both Adams came to see slavery as a great moral evil. In addition to never owning slaves, John Adams never hired slaves for temporary work.[168] That sort of thing was done in the North and the South in this era.

Abigail was not just morally repulsed by slavery, she was also irritated by its economic backwardness. From her point of view, unmotivated slaves and lazy owners could not compete with hardworking New Englanders. Interestingly, she also expressed the thought that the slaves she encountered were smarter than poor southern whites.[169] Perhaps she was engaged in rhetorical excess, but it was still an interesting thought to express, given the racism so prevalent in the South and North.

The story of John Adams and race would not be complete, however, without the inclusions of one particularly troublesome event. Adams was risked his standing in colonial public opinion by defending the Redcoats who participated in the Boston Massacre.[170] In his role as defense attorney of the Redcoats, Adams offered an unflattering picture

---

[165] Kenneth O'Reilly, *Nixon's Piano* (New York: Free Press, 1996), 18.
[166] Meacham, 45.
[167] Ellis, 9, 104.
[168] McCullough, 134.
[169] Ibid., 553.
[170] More about which will be discussed in the section on Adams' leadership.

of the mob that provoked them. He referred to the colonists involved in the altercation as "a motley rabble of saucy boys, Negroes and mulattoes, Irish teagues, and outlandish jack tars."[171] In his description, "negroes and mulattoes" is apparently alarming enough that the terms need no inflammatory adjectives. Was Adams personally a racist, or was he playing to the prejudices of the jury? Did this display a lifelong bigotry that he would carry into the White House, or was it a manifestation of the arrogant foolishness of youth?

Actions speak louder than words, and Adams acquitted himself well here. As president, Adams invited to dinner a representative of Haitian slave rebellion leader Toussaint L'Ouverture. It was the first time an American president had invited someone of African descent to dinner,[172] and it would not happen again until Theodore Roosevelt made the same invitation to Booker T. Washington. Between this gesture on the part of Adams, and his success in ridding Massachusetts of slavery, overall Adams has much to be proud of when it comes to his handling of the race issue.

During Adams' presidency, he wrote a letter to George Washington, saying that "The prosperity of (Adams' administration) will depend upon Heaven, and very little on anything in my power."[173] Do sentiments such as these cast Adams as humble and pious, a timid leader, or some combination thereof? It could have simply been a little conversational rhetoric to prompt Washington to expound upon what he felt about his own presidency. At the time, the men were in a unique fraternity; they were the only two Presidents of the United States.

Unfortunately, the personality traits that drove Adams to be a leader, also threatened to undermine his chances of being successful at it. The *John Adams Autobiography* provides some insight into the second president's character. That he cared about his reputation is obvious. This autobiography, which is really just a recounting of his role during the days of the Continental Congress, is peppered with references to rivals who do not like him for reasons that leave him

---

[171] AJ Langguth, *Patriots* (New York: Touchstone, 1989), 159.
[172] McCullough, 519.
[173] Ibid, 527.

totally mystified. He also points out several occasions where there is nothing written in the official record regarding his noteworthy contributions on a given issue. [174] But Adams was aware of his faults to a degree. He once observed that, "Vanity, I am sensible, is my cardinal folly." He was also the victim of his own passionate temper which caused, in the words of Ellis, "periodic bursts of vanity, insecurity, and sheer explosiveness."[175]

While he may have played the leader on many stages in life, Adams did not achieve such status through personal charisma. As biographer McCullough puts it, "John Adams was not a man of the world. He enjoyed no social standing. He was an awkward dancer and poor at cards. He never learned to flatter."[176] More succinctly, one might say that Adams was not a man with whom one would want to be stuck in an elevator.

Adams's lack of charisma was partially offset by his brilliance and integrity. Surprisingly, he was also considered a better public speaker than Washington or Jefferson.[177] Such a ranking put him ahead of Madison, too. All those years of arguing cases in court apparently served Adams well.

Adams' philosophy on leadership was fascinating. As Edel notes, Adams was a gifted politician with a well-deserved reputation for getting the results he wanted both in the national and international arenas. The man knew how to figure out his goals and achieve them, but Adams also "stressed that it was more honorable to be on the unpopular side of an issue."[178] Adams knew how to be a difference maker politically, but he did not want to fit into the mold of a craven, glory-seeking politician who put popularity above character. This was noble, but it resulted in Adams relishing conflict seemingly just for the

---

[174] Charles Francis Adams, Editor, *John Adams Autobiography* (Amazon Digital Services, 1850), 82-84, Kindle.
[175] Ellis, 11-12.
[176] McCullough, 19.
[177] Richard Brookhiser, *George Washington on Leadership* (New York: Perseus Books Group, 2009.), 179.
[178] Edel, 51.

sake of being contentious. And he urged his most famous son to be the same way.

Of course, this mindset helped Adams do the right thing when it came to the so-called Boston Massacre. A colonial mob was whipped into a frenzy and began harassing then attacking some Redcoats who were on guard duty a few years before the Revolutionary War. The Redcoats opened fire on people who did not have guns, and a few Americans were killed. Adams decided to defend the Redcoats when they were put on trial. Adams did this because he thought even British soldiers deserved a fair hearing. It was a risky move, though, because the Redcoats were as unpopular as Adams was ambitious. Ultimately, though, the citizens of Massachusetts admired Adams's integrity.[179]

Edel describes John Adams and John Quincy Adams alike as having "a short temper, an inclination toward opposition, a tendency to see those who differed from (them) as enemies, and an overly developed capacity for reflection and depression." But John Adams also knew how to be an encourager—at least for John Quincy. John and Abigail's standards were high, but when those standards were met, the first vice president knew how to say so. Responding to notes John Quincy sent regarding his insights on European affairs, the father writes, "I am delighted with your facts, your opinions, your principles, and your feelings."[180] Specific and detailed praise is a trait of inspiring leadership.

As a diplomat in France during the Revolutionary War, Adams was both disgusted by and jealous of Ben Franklin. Franklin's work habits were no match for those of the ultra-driven Adams. More galling than Franklin's relative laziness and indifference to the standards of their shared Puritan heritage was the fact that the French adored him. Adams had trouble making friends even in his own country, thus as Joseph J. Ellis puts it, "the jealousy was palpable."[181]

Despite finishing second in the hearts of the French, Adams was a great diplomat. Somehow, though, for all of his diplomatic success, the man could be quite clueless in interpersonal relations. For example,

---

[179] Ellis, 25-26.
[180] Edel, 53, 79.
[181] Ellis, 77.

he sent a journal to the Continental Congress detailing his work in Europe, and he included a quotation by one of his counterparts saying that Adams was the George Washington of diplomacy. It was a wonderful compliment, but Adams repeating such a remark about himself did not impress the Congress; it provoked the members to laughter.[182]

When Adams became president, he was going to bring his son home from a diplomatic pots to avoid accusations of nepotism, but Washington talked Adams out of it, noting John Quincy's valuable service. Interestingly, Adams was attacked for plotting to have his son succeed him. John Quincy's career became ammunition for the argument that the elder Adams was trying to establish a monarchy in the United States.[183] Good leaders cannot afford the luxury of being oblivious to public perceptions. Adams should have trusted his instincts, even over those of Washington.

The reality that Adams thought of himself in such grandiose terms, and his desire that the young American republic use lofty titles for its leaders, helped create a perception of Adams as a man who would be king.[184] Sadly, this attitude, coupled with his unfortunate girth would prompt the nickname "His Rotundity" to be directed at the second president.

Unfortunately for Adams, his writings on the nature of power and the ubiquity of elites in every society allowed his critics to paint him as a monarchist.[185] This was not true, exactly, but Adams could be a little tone deaf when it came to the reactions he was capable of eliciting. Especially because, though he might not have been a monarchist, he really was an elitist. In fairness to Adams, Ralph Ketcham argues that what Adams really advocated were the positives that an elite upbringing could provide. Someone born of wealth was more likely to travel and appreciate different points of view, get a superior education, receive more rigorous religious instruction, and

---

[182] Ellis, 102.
[183] Ibid., 182-183, 223.
[184] Ibid., 146.
[185] Ibid., 135.

develop an appreciation for family. These qualities would certainly be good to have among government officials.[186]

Adams' belief that men "need to be considered, esteemed, praised, beloved, and admired by his fellows"[187] tells the reader more about Adams personally than it does about humanity in general.

It is a testament to Adams' reputation as an honest and intelligent leader that he was chosen to write the Massachusetts state constitution, as mentioned above.

While Adams wanted to lead as evenhandedly as Washington, it is incumbent upon a leader to surround himself/herself with reliable people, and Adams failed to do that. In fairness, he was in uncharted waters when he became the first person to succeed a president. There was no precedent for the new chief executive to get his own people in his Cabinet, so Adams invited Washington's men to stay. Unfortunately they did, and they were not so much Washington's people as they were Alexander Hamilton's. Though Hamilton had long since left Washington's Cabinet, Hamilton still considered himself the head of the Federalist Party, and he saw Adams as too moderate and accommodating towards the opposition. Thus, Adams' Cabinet was more loyal to Hamilton than they were to their new president.

Ketcham suggests that what one might call weak or ineffectual leadership was simply Adams being loyal to his convictions. The second president would not be the champion of his party against the Democratic-Republicans, nor would he punish disloyal Federalists by kicking them out of his Cabinet. He refused to chart either course because, as Ketcham puts it, "such were certain paths to corruption and tyranny."[188]

Such a lofty view of Adams is undermined by the reality of the Alien and Sedition Acts passed in the Federalist-dominated Congress and signed into law by Adams. This series of four laws made it easier for the government to shut down opposition voices through jail times and banishment. It was effective, but it did show little regard for the

---

[186] Ketcham, 95.
[187] Ellis, 147.
[188] Ketcham, 98.

First Amendment. Ketcham dismisses this development as "only a temporary deviation from (Adams') strict respect for civil liberties."[189]

Adams' handling of the Alien and Sedition Acts underscores his ineffectual leadership. Adams was reluctant to enforce the acts,[190] which made sense given that they violated his principles. But signing them into law offended one party and not enforcing them with vigor disappointed the other. Adams' efforts to find a middle path left him isolated,

Surrounded by pawns of Alexander Hamilton, Adams frequently felt alone in office. After putting up with their disloyalties and Hamilton's schemes for too long, Adams finally blew up and fired one of his Cabinet officers, James McHenry. Adams had waited almost his entire term in office to do it, so as a practical matter it was rather pointless. Worse yet, because the infamous Adams' temper had been bottled up too long, he erupted with such ferocity that McHenry told a relative that Adams was "actually insane."[191]

The mental illness story had legs. The accusation would re-appear during the Election of 1800. Of course, Democratic-Republican attack dogs also accused Adams of being a womanizer,[192] which was ridiculous. Part of the high price of leadership, though, is that people will attack you unfairly. Newspapermen, including James Callender, wrote horrible things about the second president, like saying Adams was a "hideous hermaphroditical character (with) neither the force and firmness of a man, nor the gentleness and sensibility of a woman."[193]

McCullough points out that Adams did not fund those kinds of attacks on political enemies, but Jefferson did.[194] Of course, Adams did not have to fund such attacks, if he could throw those who made them in jail.

---

[189] Ketcham, 99.
[190] Bernard A. Weisberger, *America Afire: Jefferson, Adams, and the Revolutionary Election of 1800* (New York: William Morrow, 2000), 212.
[191] McCullough, 538.
[192] Ibid., 544.
[193] McCullough, 537.
[194] Ibid., 536.

When France began attacking American ships in an effort to undermine Britain's economy during one of the frequent wars in Europe, many in America called for a declaration of war against France in the 1790s. Adams settled for a Quasi War—an undeclared naval confrontation. The fledgling United States navy acquitted itself well, primarily because France was preoccupied with Britain. Adams was satisfied with a relatively quick peace treaty rather than pressing the Americans' advantage and gaining more at the negotiating table while prolonging the war. Adams saved lives but defied key members of his political party in doing so. Historian Edel believes that Adams lost his re-election bid in 1800 because this policy decision hurt his support so much among Federalists.[195]

Adams' efforts at strong leadership were not just undermined by a disloyal Cabinet, he was in the uniquely awkward position of having a vice president who was in a different political party. Adams was a Federalist; Thomas Jefferson was a Democratic-Republican. Adams thought he could bridge this divide because of his friendship with Jefferson, and because it was best for the country. Adams wanted either Jefferson or the VP's right hand man James Madison to be intimately involved with foreign policy. Jefferson said no thanks, but there was more to it than that. The vice president of the United States actually encouraged the French to ignore any peace overtures from Adams. Historian Ellis says this "verged on treason."[196] One could easily argue that it moved past verging. Adams might be recognized as a more successful leader today, if not for the betrayal of Thomas Jefferson.

Yet another factor that worked against Adams as a leader was his lack of true leadership experience. Washington had commanded an army, and Jefferson had been Governor of Virginia. These were life experiences that Adams did not have. Perhaps if he had been in charge of such large groups of people, Ellis theorizes, Adams would have gotten over peculiar ideas like, for example, a policy must be good if it was unpopular.[197]

---

[195] Edel, 87.
[196] Ellis, 175-177.
[197] Ibid., 181.

In 1820, twenty years after completing one miserable term as president before being voted out, Adams was invited to a Massachusetts state constitutional convention to revise the constitution, the one Adams had written almost by himself. Adams offered little input to the proceedings, but he did suggest that they remove any religious qualifications for voting. Interestingly, the assembly voted him down. Perhaps even more interestingly, Adams other comment was that they should maintain property ownership as a requirement for voting, and he was voted down on that, too.[198] In the end, the man who wanted to make an impact found that he had no influence. But being there to discuss the document he wrote virtually single-handedly was a reminder of Adams' talent and the trust his fellow citizens had in his character.

John Adams was an interesting figure. He was a faithful churchgoer and defender of the Bible who nevertheless had heterodox views. He spent a virtual lifetime in leadership positions, yet he was unable to manage the office of the president with success. But in the third area of our study, Adams was peerless. His role in rooting slavery out of Massachusetts before it ever gained much of a foothold guaranteed that this state would not subjugate future generations of men, women, and children. It also helped to set a moral standard for several other states that were seriously considering the idea of putting slavery on the road to extinction. Thus, one could argue that Adams improved the lives of more African Americans—then and in subsequent generations—than the other presidents in this study. Despite the long shadows of Washington, Jefferson, and Franklin, John Adams finally finished first at something!

---

[198] Ellis, 248.

CHAPTER 5

#3 THOMAS JEFFERSON

Thomas Jefferson is a much more controversial figure than many Americans realize today. On the one hand, he possessed a brilliant mind, an ability to inspire large groups, and a charisma that drew individuals to him. Unfortunately, that is not the whole story. His inconsistency of character has already been touched on, and in this chapter it will be seen even more vividly, specifically as it relates to his religious beliefs, his views on African Americans, and the leadership principles that guided his behavior. Interestingly, his greatest consistency comes through on the religion question.

Part of the challenge in understanding Thomas Jefferson is that the man made himself so hard to read. Case in point: Jefferson faced a unique difficulty at one stage of his political career—he was a member of the Democratic-Republican Party while serving as vice president for a Federalist president. Jefferson had been a long-time friend of this president, John Adams, but obviously their political philosophies were different. Adams thought that he could trust Jefferson as a friend, but Jefferson was working against him. Perhaps Adams was naïve, but in his defense, as author Jim Cullen points out, "Jefferson never announced his position—he hated personal confrontation and would rather dissemble than face acrimony."[199]

Cullen goes on to write that Jefferson "had a restless mind that could stray remarkably, even alarmingly, far from pragmatic

---

[199] Jim Cullen, *Imperfect Presidents* (New York: Fall River Press, 2007), 26.

considerations." For example, the author cites the lifelong slaveholding Jefferson writing "all men are created equal." As Cullen cleverly puts it, "The complexities of lived experience were elusive, if not repugnant, to him."[200] In short, Jefferson was a man of contradictions, so when Adams found that Jefferson was both his friend and his betrayer, this inconsistency was not a unique circumstance in Jefferson's life.

The most passionate defense of Thomas Jefferson's character and faith comes from David Barton, whose book *The Jefferson Lies* claims to set the record straight against all of the secular historians who have portrayed the third president as an atheist who hated African Americans, thought they were inherently inferior, and fathered several children with his slave Sally Hemings. Barton focuses on these accusations and more before concluding that "Jefferson was not a secularist, Deist, or atheist." Actually, Jefferson was "a Christian Primitivist, being in personal disagreement with some orthodox theological tenets of Christianity that he had affirmed earlier in life." Finally, "there was never a time in his life when Jefferson was not pro-Christian and pro-Christianity."[201]

These are interesting assertions for Barton to make, given the sentiments of others who have studied the third president. Evangelical authors Peter Marshall and David Manuel characterize Jefferson as a man with, as they word it, "no personal knowledge" of God. As part of their argument, they quote a letter Jefferson wrote to John Adams, which says, "The day will come when the mystical generation of Jesus, by the supreme being of his father and the womb of a virgin, will be classed with the fable of the generation of Minerva in the brain of Jupiter."[202] Christine Leigh Heyrman says, Jefferson "dismissed the Bible as a collection of myths and derided the notion of a trinity as 'Abracadabra.'" He encouraged his daughters and his nephew Peter

---

[200] Cullen, 27.
[201] David Barton, *The Jefferson Lies* (Nashville: Thomas Nelson, 2012), 4357-4362, Kindle.
[202] Peter Marshall and David Manuel, *From Sea to Shining Sea* (Grand Rapids: Fleming H. Revell, 1986), 111.

Carr to feel free to question everything even "with boldness...the existence of a god."[203]

Did Thomas Jefferson believe in the power of prayer? Well, he did once write to Madison regarding Patrick Henry, "What we have to do, I think, is devoutly...pray for his death." Jefferson was kidding, but the real irony of it was that the issue at hand involved the separation of church and state in Virginia.[204]

Alf J. Mapp, Jr. raises an excellent point when he says that when some believe Jefferson is contradicting himself on religion, they fail to account for his views evolving over time. Jefferson was not a hypocrite, argues Mapp; the third president simply changed his mind on some things as he acquired more life experience.[205] Really, the age question is one to keep in mind when looking at the faith of any historical figure.

Jefferson was certainly not a lifelong enemy of all things religious. As a child, he used to enjoy singing psalms with his sister, Jane, but Jefferson had another childhood memory that was not so positive. During school hours, he sometimes hid and recited the Lord's Prayer, somehow believing this might cause the school day to end more quickly. It never worked.[206]

As a young man, Jefferson read Lord Bolingbroke, whose vision of the patriot king inspired many of the Founders. Jefferson was not only interested in Bolingbroke's politics, though; Jefferson was also intrigued by how Bolingbroke favored Deism over traditional Christianity.[207]

Jefferson wrote a resolution calling for a day of prayer and fasting in 1774, but by his own admission this was something he

---

[203] Christine L. Heyrman, *Southern Cross* (Chapel Hill: North Carolina Press, 1997), 7.

[204] Jon Meacham, *American Gospel* (New York: Random House, 2007), 84-85.

[205] Alf J. Mapp, Jr., *The Faith of our Fathers* (New York: Fall River Press, 2006), 17-18.

[206] Jon Meacham, *Thomas Jefferson* (New York: Random House, 2012), 10, 13.

[207] Ralph Ketcham, *Presidents above Party* (Chapel Hill: University of North Carolina Press, 1984), 100; Meacham (2012), 28.

"cooked up" for the purpose of "arousing our people from the lethargy into which they had fallen." Author Steven Waldman feels that this smacks of cynicism, and it is easy to agree with him.[208] In fact, as mentioned in the last chapter, Jefferson had also opposed the call for a day of fasting that someone else had presented in the Congress, and Jefferson drew a rebuke from John Adams for it.[209]

The election in 1800 between Jefferson and Adams was the first presidential contest in which religion arose as an issue. Critics accused Jefferson of being an atheist, and author Bernard A. Weisberger has an interesting theory as to why this occurred when it did. No one complained about Jefferson's faith when George Washington picked him to be the first secretary of state twelve years earlier. Weisberger believes that the problem was Jefferson's support for the French Revolutionaries. There was quite a bit of fluidity among the leadership in France, and a group had risen to power that was hostile to religion. Since Jefferson had supported the revolutionaries, political opponents in America made the connection between the revolutionaries' attitude about faith and Jefferson's own. One alarmed American wrote that if the supposedly anti-religious Jefferson was elected, men would start getting killed and women and girls would be seduced because the moral restraints of religion would be lost. One Federalist asked, "Shall I continue in allegiance to God and a religious president, or simply declare for Jefferson—and no God?"[210]

Jefferson was accused by one northern minister of being a "howling atheist."[211] Others feared that "if Jefferson were elected, he would confiscate all Bibles and turn churches into temples of prostitution."[212] Indeed, such were the persistent fears of Jefferson's religion that he felt compelled to assure Connecticut Baptists that he was no threat to their faith in his 1802 message where he famously

[208] Steven Waldman, *Founding Faith* (New York: Random House, 2008), 71.
[209] David McCullough *John Adams* (New York: Touchstone Books, 2002), 113.
[210] Bernard A. Weisberger, *America Afire: Jefferson, Adams, and the Revolutionary Election of 1800* (New York: William Morrow, 2000), 251.
[211] John Seigenthaler, *James K. Polk* (New York: Henry Holt and Company, 2004), 13.
[212] Mapp, 3.

referred to "building a wall of separation between Church and State."[213] Though the phrase today is often used to push against expressions of religious faith in the public sphere, it was meant at the time to reassure the faithful that the government would not be a threat to their free expression or religious liberty.

The persistence of the religion question in Jefferson's lifetime is rather remarkable. It came up again when Thomas Paine visited America while Jefferson was president. For Jefferson, welcoming Paine's return was a humanitarian gesture to a hero of the American Revolution; Paine's life was threatened by France's revolution. But a Baltimore newspaper described it differently, sarcastically stating, "Our pious President thought it expedient to dispatch a frigate for the accommodation of this loathsome reptile." Why the vitriol? As Joseph J. Ellis so colorfully puts it, "Paine's chief offense was not that he was a practicing alcoholic with the social graces of a derelict, though that was true, but rather that he had written *The Age of Reason*, which was as full-throated an attack on Christianity as *Common Sense* had been on monarchy."[214] In the end, Jefferson gave in to the pressure to disassociate himself from the offer of free passage for Paine.[215]

Jefferson weighed in on the topic of faith in a letter to James Fishback in 1809. The now-retired president argued that all religions agree on "moral precepts." Thus, they were all useful when it came to promoting an orderly society. But, he went on, there was a problem regarding dogmas. On such things as the divinity of Christ, the Virgin Birth, an appropriate method for baptism, etc., the religions disagreed, and much blood had been spilled. Jefferson thought it would be best if people would just "be quiet on these speculations."[216] While this would have been a great way to avoid religious arguments, one is hard pressed to maintain that Jefferson was a Christian when he wished people would not discuss the deity of Christ.

---

[213] Meacham (2007), 104-105.

[214] Joseph J. Ellis, *American Sphinx* (New York: Vintage Books, 1998), 257.

[215] Marshall and Manuel, 111.

[216] J. Jefferson Looney, Editor, *The Papers of Thomas Jefferson*, Volume 1, (Princeton: Princeton University Press, 2004), 563-564.

Of course, Jefferson being Jefferson, after writing this candid appraisal of his beliefs, he wrote a second version of the letter, which was shorter and less forthcoming. He sent the second letter and sat on the first one.[217]

Jefferson was invited to be a godfather but declined, he writes, because he did not believe in the Trinity, so he could not take the oath required by the church. In contrast Washington served as the godfather for eight children over the years without making an issue over the oaths.[218]

Steven Waldman tries to find a middle ground for Jefferson, somewhere between Barton and, well, everybody else. Waldman uses the story of Jefferson editing the miracles out of the Bible to help make his case. The author accuses evangelicals of spreading the story that Jefferson did this simply to try and civilize the Native Americans.[219] The problem, though, is that Waldman does nothing to discredit the argument, other than trying to reduce it in status by declaring it a rumor. Curiously, evangelical writers Marshall and Manuel claim the edited Bible by Jefferson was supposed to be for his children, though they, too, are lacking in supporting material.[220] Waldman takes exception to the idea that the Jefferson Bible proves that the third president was a secularist. Instead, Waldman argues that Jefferson was a man who loved Jesus as an ethical teacher. Thus, Jefferson was trying to rescue the historical Jesus from "ignorant, unlettered men," which was Jefferson's description of the Gospel writers. Jefferson was not trying to ignore Jesus, like the secularists; Jefferson was trying to save Him.[221] Cullen has a different take on this. He believes that such an effort by the third president "suggests that his celebrated invocations of religious tolerance were little more than evidence of his detachment, even indifference, towards the complexities of spiritual life."[222]

---

[217] Looney, Volume 1, 563, 565-566.
[218] Thompson, 33 -35.
[219] Steven Waldman, *Founding Faith* (New York: Random House, 2008), 72.
[220] Marshall and Manuel, 111.
[221] Waldman, 73.
[222] Cullen, 27.

In a letter to John Adams, Jefferson writes on the subject of the universe, "It is impossible for the human mind not to perceive and feel a conviction of design, consummate skill, and indefinite power in every atom of its composition." This led Waldman to say, "Yes, Thomas Jefferson—hero of modern liberals—believed in intelligent design"[223] Of course, in and of itself, this simply makes Jefferson a believer in some kind of Higher Power, not a Christian.

A problem for evangelicals when trying to claim Jefferson as one of their own is something the man said while in France, the birthplace of the Enlightenment. Jefferson remarked, "It does me no injury for my neighbor to say there are twenty gods, or no God. It neither picks my pocket nor breaks my leg."[224] Even if Jefferson was simply trying to make a legal or philosophical point in favor of religious liberty, his argument should be a little unsettling for an orthodox believer. If Jefferson was a Christian then Jefferson should be troubled by his polytheistic or atheistic neighbors. The thought of their eternal damnation should trouble anyone who followed the Christ who gave His disciples the Great Commission to share their faith to the ends of the earth.

A biographer approached Jefferson late in life and asked if he had changed his beliefs, as some were saying of him. Jefferson first pointed out that the people talking about him that way did not really know what his beliefs were before. He told the biographer to "say nothing of my religion. It is known to my god and myself alone." While Jefferson was not exactly letting his light shine here, he was more candid with John Adams. Jefferson suggested that Adams' theology to simply "be just and good" was where religious "enquiries must end." Jefferson thought that where religions agreed they were probably right, and where they disagreed they were probably wrong.[225] This sounds pretty tolerant, but there is nothing about it that one could fit within a traditional, orthodox understanding of Christianity.

---

[223] Waldman, 83-84.

[224] Meacham (2007), 85.

[225] Jefferson wrote all of this in a letter to John Adams dated January 11, 1817. J. Jefferson Looney, Editor, *The Papers of Thomas Jefferson*, Volume 10, (Princeton: Princeton University Press, 2013), 658.

In an 1822 letter to Adams, Jefferson said, "I trust that there is not a young man now living in the US who will not die a Unitarian."[226] Jefferson also said that if he were starting a new religion, he would decree "that we are to be saved by our good works, which are within our power, and not by our faith, which is not within our power."[227]

Despite what Barton argues, the evidence indicates that Jefferson had little respect for the orthodox views of Christianity, and he tended to be cynical regarding religious leaders. Of the six men in this study, he had the lowest opinion of Christianity, and his views were the most contrary to its doctrines.

In his efforts to rehabilitate Jefferson's image relative to the slavery issue, Barton argues that Jefferson was a lifelong champion of better treatment for African Americans. Also, he wanted to end slavery, but he did not have the legal flexibility that George Washington possessed just a few years earlier.[228]

On the other hand, Garry Wills, among others, points out that when the nation began to expand in a southwesterly direction, Jefferson was one of the advocates for slavery expanding with it. Wills did not think Jefferson was motivated so much by notions of racial superiority as he was by wanting to extend the political and economic influence of those supporting the southern way of life.[229] Jefferson is just not quite the moral and ethical hero on slavery that Barton tries to make him out to be. That said, Jefferson was not just a villain either.

Jefferson's work in the early 1780s entitled *Notes on the State of Virginia*, stated that people of African descent were simply biologically inferior.[230] This could be seen as an attempt to justify slavery, but on the other hand—and of course with Jefferson there was frequently another hand—Jefferson also expresses his discomfort with slavery and its negative effects on both the enslaved and the enslavers.[231]

---

[226] Thomas Jefferson *Memoir, Correspondence* (Alexandria, VA: The Library of Alexandria, 2008), Kindle. L 35776-35800.

[227] Meacham (2012), 471.

[228] Barton, L 2190-2320.

[229] Garry Wills, *Negro President* (Boston: Houghton Mifflin, 2003), 9.

[230] Ellis (2010), 127-128.

It would be tempting to portray Jefferson as a hypocrite on this topic because he does argue from both sides over the course of his career; and, of course, on other occasions the man is a hypocrite, but the truth can be a complicated thing. People tend to remember that Jefferson wrote "all men are created equal," but this was not the only time he pushed in the direction of a post-slavery society.

In 1769, Jefferson actually argued before the Virginia House of Burgesses on behalf of emancipation, but he was rebuffed.[232] Jefferson was not exactly relentless on the issue, but in his younger and perhaps more idealistic days, the man tried.

As a member of the Virginia Legislature during the Revolutionary era, Jefferson was a champion for liberty in a variety of spheres including criminal justice, education, and religion in addition to his work on slavery. There was a consistent theme of freedom at work here. Jefferson and others had called for a plan that had worked in ending slavery in several states in the North. After a certain date, set several years in the future, anyone born in Virginia would automatically be free. The Virginians' plan featured an additional caveat—the ex-slaves would be deported. The notion that whites and non-whites could not conceivably participate equally and peacefully in society was not just a southern idea, but it was a more pressing one there because African Americans existed in such large numbers. Ultimately, though, it was a moot point because, as mentioned above, the legislators rejected Jefferson's plans for ending slavery.[233]

Jefferson might have wanted to better the circumstances of the slaves at some future point, but there is also documentation that he was willing to sell a slave to settle a debt.[234] This was something other owners, like Washington and Madison, avoided doing. Many owners saw themselves as benevolent figures, and selling a slave to someone else meant that the slave was no longer under such caring protection. Jefferson was apparently not bound by this ethic.

---

[231] McCullough, 134.

[232] Jefferson, L 99-103.

[233] Meacham (2012), 121-124.

[234] J. Jefferson Looney, Editor, *The Papers of Thomas Jefferson,* Volume 9, (Princeton, NJ: Princeton University press, 2012), 215-216.

When he was working on the Declaration of Independence with John Adams, Ben Franklin, and the rest of their committee, Jefferson included language that was critical of slavery. The Continental Congress called for the removal of this passage along with other edits—a process that irritated Jefferson greatly.[235] In the end, the only line that could even be potentially construed as anti-slavery was the one regarding the equality of men. It was an important, genuinely revolutionary line, but Jefferson had wanted an even stronger statement against slavery.

When it came to the admission of new states in the North, Jefferson proposed in 1784 that slavery should be outlawed there.[236] Perhaps he was committed to fairness here, or he was following a pattern of encouraging an idealistically high standard for others that would not disrupt his personal circumstances at all. Both might be true.

In a letter dated September 16, 1816, Jefferson refers to the legality of slavery as "the unfortunate state of things with us."[237] Nevertheless, four years later he was offering unconvincing rationalizations for spreading slavery into Missouri and beyond. According to the Virginian, those of African descent could handle working in the hot sun more easily than whites could, Africans did not need as much rest, the men had less genuine love for their women, they handled grief more easily than whites, and slaves were not as smart as their masters anyway.[238] In short, slavery was not so bad after all, according to Jefferson.

Finally, at his death he did not free his slaves in his will, even though he had no widow left behind to take into consideration.

Jefferson did not like slavery, especially earlier in life, but he became a proponent of its expansion deeper into the country. His efforts to rationalize sound rather desperate. On this issue, Jefferson the idealist was no match for Jefferson the pragmatist.

---

[235] Meacham (2012), 105-106.

[236] Harlow Giles Unger, *The Last Founding Father* (Philadelphia: Da Capo, 2010), 60.

[237] Looney, Volume 10, 368.

[238] Thomas Jefferson *Notes on the State of Virginia* Kindle Loc. 2430-2436.

What kind of leader was Jefferson? According to Jon Meacham, who wrote a book on Jefferson's leadership, the third president "liked to cultivate the air of a philosopher who was above the merely political." Jefferson did not always succeed at this, but it was his goal. Meacham also says that Jefferson "was raised to wield power...he was taught that to be great...one had to grow comfortable with authority and with responsibility.[239]

In his eight years as president, Jefferson was popular for substantially reducing the national debt, cutting taxes, and doubling the size of the country without firing a shot thanks to the Louisiana Purchase. Of course, paying for Louisiana raised the debt, but one cannot have everything. Also, purchasing land was not a power explicitly given to the federal government by the Constitution, so it was the sort of thing that contradicted Jefferson's political principles, but as usual, many people were willing to look the other way when it came to Jefferson's hypocrisy.

From Jefferson's election as president in 1800 until 1840, Meacham points out, every president was either "a self-described adherent of his," Jefferson himself, or John Quincy Adams.[240] Quincy Adams was not a disciple of Jefferson's politically-speaking, but the sixth president only served four years. And despite their differences Jefferson had been a mentor to the younger Adams while they were in France. [241] Thus, Meacham's premise is correct—Jefferson was remarkably influential over the White House for almost a half century.

Jefferson could be eloquent in print, but he usually avoided writing about political issues in newspapers, which many of his political contemporaries and successors did. One historian is rather charitable in his explanation for this, saying "shyness held him back; so did a combination of patience and optimism: he always suspected he would be on the winning side, and he was often right."[242] Perhaps this

---

[239] Meacham (2012), xviii, 4.
[240] Ibid., xix.
[241] Charles N. Edel, *Nation Builder* (Cambridge, MA: Harvard University Press, 2014) 35.
[242] Richard Brookhiser, *George Washington on Leadership* (New York: Perseus Books Group, 2009), 209.

is the correct interpretation, but it also could be argued that Jefferson did not want to be pinned down by his own words when he could get someone else to do his dirty work.

Brookhiser explains Jefferson's penchant for saying one thing and doing another as a manifestation of Jefferson's dislike of confrontation. Brookhiser believes that Jefferson simply "tended to overcompensate" when he had a disagreement, "appearing to agree with whomever he was with."[243]

Perhaps one of the most egregious examples of Jefferson's duplicity, and one that Brookhiser's formula does not cover, is found in Jefferson's financial support for a partisan hack, James Callender who wrote terrible things, many of them totally fictitious, about Washington, Adams, and Hamilton. Then, Jefferson denied he had done so.[244] As Jefferson told Monroe when Jefferson was funding all sorts of attacks—some bizarrely personal—against John Adams in the Election of 1800, "Do not let my name be connected with the business."[245]

Johnstone seems a little too charitable regarding Jefferson when referencing the issue of Jefferson and the highly partisan press. Jefferson's personal code, character, and "hatred of controversy" conspired to prevent him from "exploiting (newspapers) to the fullest extent," but Johnstone concedes Jefferson still managed to exploit them more than any of his contemporaries.[246] So what is the takeaway here? Was Jefferson a model of restraint when it came to exploiting attack dogs in the press, or was he the worst offender? In fact, Johnstone seems to concede the argument later in his book when he writes, "Jefferson and his party colleagues made what might be considered optimum use of the press as they sought to disseminate political intelligence and mobilize partisan loyalties."[247]

---

[243] Brookhiser, 79.
[244] Ellis (2010), 230.
[245] McCullough, 536.
[246] Robert M. Johnstone, Jr., Robert M. *Jefferson and the presidency* (Ithaca: Cornell University Press, 1978), 243.
[247] Ibid., 250.

Yet another example of Jefferson's (lack of) integrity is seen in his handling of a review of Thomas Paine's *The Rights of Man*. While praising the book, Jefferson criticized Adams for the second president's supposed monarchical tendencies. Jefferson thought his review would be anonymous. When it turned out that it was not, Adams confronted Jefferson, who lied and said that his criticism was not aimed at Adams.[248]

Jefferson might have had, as Ketcham says, a "nonpartisan conception of executive leadership," but he apparently did not feel the same way about the office of secretary of state. Or, perhaps his belief that Washington was becoming a tool of the Federalists[249] compelled Jefferson to lead the Democratic-Republican Party against him. After Washington decided that the United States should stay neutral during the French Revolution, the pro-peasant, Francophile Jefferson coached the French ambassador, Edmond Genet, on how to circumvent American neutrality. John Adams had a theory on why the secretary of state was trying secretly to undermine his own administration. Jefferson, like a lot of Virginia planters, owed a great amount of money to British banks. Helping France and undermining Britain served Jefferson's personal interests.[250] Even when Jefferson gave up on Genet, it was not out of deference to the president, who was Jefferson's boss. It was because, as Jefferson admitted to Madison, it had become clear that Genet was destined for a bad end, and Jefferson did not want to be tainted by association.[251]

To Jefferson's credit, he was not too proud of a leader to admit when he had made a mistake. He observed to his friend, turned enemy, turned friend again John Adams that Jefferson's view of revolutionary France had been inferior to the second president's. The relationship of the United States with Britain and France had been the biggest foreign policy concern of both of their presidencies, and Jefferson admitted that Adams had gotten it right, but Jefferson had not. That was gracious.[252]

---

[248] Ellis (2010) 153-154.
[249] Ketcham, 102.
[250] Ellis (2010), 165-166.
[251] Ellis (1998), 150.
[252] Ellis (2010), 239.

Historian Robert M. Johnstone, Jr. makes an interesting point about Jefferson as a leader: the third president basically made his office the head of the government. The Framers of the Constitution had reacted against the memory of a heavy handed British monarchy when they clearly delineated a separation of powers. Congress had a set of responsibilities—creating legislation, setting budgets, etc.—that the president was not supposed to influence. Washington was too aloof and detached to cross those boundaries, and Adams was too personally irritating to get away with it. Also, Adams, like Washington, was committed to rising above partisanship. But Jefferson had control of a political party. It was in that position as party leader, according to Johnstone, that Jefferson was able to put his stamp on the government and make the president its head. It took all of Jefferson's charm, intellect, and party connections, but he did it.[253]

Jefferson seemed to genuinely believe—if one is ever comfortable using the word "genuinely" in relation to the third president—that Federalists and Democratic-Republicans could come together under his leadership.[254] He was more partisan than Washington and Adams, but he was not as partisan as the modern presidents. Jefferson pushed legislation through Congress with the help of his political party's dominance. Jefferson accomplished this with his personal charisma and by working with men of similar philosophies rather than employing the threat or reality of party discipline the way a modern chief executive would. Even so, as Ketcham writes, "The president also often cautioned the legislators to shield his role in the measures."[255] It is truly amazing how consistently secretive and misleading Jefferson was.

In Cabinet meetings, Jefferson felt that the president should have one vote. Jefferson knew that he could make decisions unilaterally, but he did not think that was prudent.[256] This sounds humble, and it was, but one should bear in mind that Jefferson

---

[253] Johnstone, Jr., 25.
[254] Ketcham, 105.
[255] Ibid., 109.
[256] Norma Lois Peterson, *The Presidencies of William Henry Harrison & John Tyler* (Lawrence: University of Kansas, 1989), 40.

surrounded himself with people who were more likely to think like he did, which Washington and Adams did not do. Also, given Jefferson's propensity for denying responsibility for controversial actions, perhaps he was just trying to protect his reputation if a policy backfired.

Jefferson could be charming with anyone, and he could be dishonest when it served his agenda, so the man knew how to keep his feelings under control. But there was one area where the third president apparently felt no need to play it cool. According to a relative, when it came to his horse, Jefferson asserted his control with "a fearless application of the whip on the slightest manifestation of restiveness."[257] What kind of man severely beats his horse for minor demonstrations of spirit? Was this assertive leadership or animal abuse?

The two sides of Jefferson ran along a line throughout his circumstances; they were not just a byproduct of his politics. How else would one explain the man's tragic personal life? His promise to his dying wife that he would never marry again is the stuff of romance novels. However, his relations with women also have a tawdry air to them. DNA evidence indicates he probably fathered several children with a slave named Sally Hemings, and then there is his pursuit of the married Elizabeth Walker. His unsuccessful efforts to seduce Mrs. Walker lasted for years and were not blunted in the least by the fact that she was married to a good friend of his. Jefferson was even a groomsman in their wedding. Finally, Jefferson had a lengthy and rather open flirtation—and perhaps more—with another married woman, Maria Cosway, while he was in France.[258]

Jefferson's earlier pursuit of Rebecca Lewis Burwell ended badly for him, but at least neither of them were married at the time. That said, he wrote in a letter to a friend something that suggested that Jefferson was coping with this setback by satisfying his sexual frustration by other means. Jefferson references St. Paul's admonition that "it is better to be married than to burn," but Jefferson writes that "providence" has provided "other means for extinguishing their fire

---

[257] McCullough, 114.
[258] Meacham (2012), 40-42, 145-146, 197-204, 507.

than those of matrimony." Meacham theorizes that Jefferson is referring to a servant or a slave.[259]

Perhaps Jefferson rationalized his behavior towards women based on his perception of their inferiority. In a December 1786 letter to his good friend Madison, Jefferson expressed a surprising concern about women. Jefferson was rightfully proud of the role he and Madison played in insuring liberty of conscience in their home state by pushing through the Virginia Statute for Religious Freedom. After praising the new law freeing people from "vassalage by kings, priests, and nobles," Jefferson turned to a different topic in the next paragraph. The future president hoped that Virginia would soften its punishment for rape. He was concerned that women might make false accusations against men who had rejected them. It was a rather bizarre issue for Jefferson to tackle, which might be why Madison chose to ignore it altogether in his reply.[260]

This was not Jefferson's only peculiar attitude involving women. He was writing about representation in Congress when he offhandedly remarked on why women could not vote. The lack of women's suffrage was necessary because in order to "prevent depravation of morals (women) could not mix promiscuously in the public meetings of men."[261] One is left to wonder if this was a common sentiment, or simply lazy writing by someone who felt the issue was so obvious that it did not need serious thought, but it seems strange today.

Whatever the third president's flaws, Ketcham characterizes Jefferson's leadership as generally brilliant.[262] Meacham writes, "Broadly put, philosophers think; politicians maneuver. Jefferson's genius was that he was both and could do both, often simultaneously. Such is the art of power."[263]

Jefferson, much like the two Adams and Madison, greatly valued the acquisition of knowledge. The third president's brilliance

---

[259] Meacham (2012), 25-26.
[260] James Morton Smith, Editor, *The Republic of Letters* (New York: W.W. Norton and Company, 1995), 459-464.
[261] Looney, Volume 10, 367-368.
[262] Ketcham, 110.
[263] Meacham (2012), xx.

prompted one of John Kennedy's most famous quotations. Surprisingly, there are different versions of what Kennedy actually said, but the gist of it was that Kennedy had brought together a group of people embodying the greatest intellectual talent ever gathered in the White House—with the possible exception of when Thomas Jefferson dined alone.

Meacham claims, "It was said that Jefferson studied fifteen hours a day." The man was full of questions, and became known as a "walking encyclopedia." Perhaps better than his peers, though, Jefferson understood that true leadership "meant knowing how to distill complexity into a comprehensible message to reach the hearts as well as the minds of the larger world," wrote Meacham.[264]

Jefferson had a kind of executive experience to draw on as president that Washington, Madison, and the two Adams lacked—Jefferson was the Governor of Virginia from 1779 to 1781. It was not the smoothest of experiences for Jefferson; he had to flee the British Army and was investigated by his legislature afterwards for incompetence. In the end, Jefferson's reputation was redeemed. His troubles were officially blamed on the inherent weakness of his office rather than bad decision-making or character flaws on Jefferson's part.

The contradictions of the man were fascinating. He claimed to respect Jesus, but he generally had a low opinion of the Church. He liked to imagine a world without slavery, yet he eventually fought for the spread of it. Despite this, Jefferson deserves high marks if one is judging him solely as a leader. He was a popular two-term president, he led his party successfully, he was brilliant, and he knew how to share credit and responsibility. The fact that the man could fashion such an impressive career and have such a tremendous impact on the country while carrying his deep personal flaws is remarkable.

---

[264] Meacham (2012), 19, 35.

CHAPTER 6

#4 JAMES MADISON

It might be tempting to consider the next set of presidents as a cut below the heroes of the Revolutionary era who became the first three chief executives. Jefferson, however, would disagree when it comes to James Madison. Jefferson once famously referred to Madison as "the greatest man in the world."[265]

Jefferson's comment leads to a couple of obvious questions for this book. What was so great about the fourth president, and what were Madison's views on faith, African Americans, and leadership?

Unlike Jefferson, James Madison was consistently sympathetic to religion. As Alf J. Mapp, Jr. writes, "In an age when some Enlightenment leaders wrote of religion as a remnant sure to retreat from the world before an advancing science, Madison's unwavering insistence on religion's eternal importance bolstered the faith of many."[266]

Madison was born into and educated by the Anglican Church.[267] When it was time for Madison to go to college, though, he did not go to Anglican-influenced William and Mary, where students and faculty

---

[265] Lynne Cheney, *James Madison* (New York: Viking, 2014), 207.

[266] In fairness, I am curious as to what evidence Mapp has that "many" had their faith bolstered by Madison. Alf J. Mapp, Jr., *The Faiths of our Founders* (New York: Fall River Press, 2006), 51.

[267] Jeff Broadwater, *James Madison* (Chapel Hill: University of North Carolina Press, 2012), 2, 5.

tended to be distracted from academics by more worldly considerations.[268] Instead, Madison headed north to Princeton, which by 1769 had become a bastion of evangelical Presbyterianism and liberal political ideology. Madison was obviously enthusiastic about the latter, and seemed pretty interested in the former, too, at least for a while.[269]

Madison was a student of theology and gave some thought to entering the ministry. His initial reason for not pursuing this course was a practical consideration rather than a theological one. He had a weak voice. His theology as a young man, though, was decidedly orthodox. He once wrote to a friend that the best kind of testimony was when the most successful men said their accomplishments left them dissatisfied, and their only solution was in "becoming fervent advocates in the cause of Christ." However, his studies at Princeton caused him to move away from his orthodox Christian theology, according to Mapp, who says the future fourth president "yielded by degrees to a growing acceptance of Deism."[270]

One might question the belief that Princeton corrupted the religious ideas of young Madison, given that he stayed there for several months after his graduation and studied Hebrew.[271] He also pursued post graduate studies in law, but one is left to wonder about his interest in Hebrew. The practical value of such work would be to prepare him for the ministry, or at least for being a better student of the Old Testament. Perhaps he thought insight into a Hebraic reading of Old Testament law would make him better able to argue English common law, but that seems like a stretch. Maybe he valued the knowledge for knowledge's sake, but it does strike one as a somewhat odd pursuit for a Deist.

A legitimate question to ask regarding Madison's spiritual journey is this: did he fall under the influence of Jefferson's heretical[272]

---

[268] Andrew Levy, *The First Emancipator* (New York: Random House, 2005), 38.

[269] Broadwater, 3.

[270] Mapp, 45-47.

[271] Broadwater, 3.

[272] I realize the term might seem inflammatory, but it is easy to argue its technical accuracy.

outlook? Lynne Cheney points out that Madison's spiritual views had already changed before he really got to know his eventual friend and mentor.[273]

Madison once corresponded with an Episcopal priest named Frederick Beasley, who was also the provost of the University of Pennsylvania. Madison wrote, "The belief in a God all powerful, wise, and good is so essential to the moral order of the world and to the happiness of man, that arguments which enforce it cannot be drawn from too many sources." Yet author David L. Holmes points out that Madison fails to use the Bible or Jesus to buttress his position, which leads Holmes, like Mapp, to the conclusion that Madison was more of a Deist than an orthodox Christian.[274] Of course, going beyond traditional sources is actually the point of what Madison was saying, so perhaps he felt that Father Beasley could make the Bible-based arguments, and Madison could focus his laser-sharp intellect along other avenues when discussing God and morality.

Madison, like his good friend Jefferson, was a Virginian who opposed the idea of an established church. He did not believe that one should have to pay taxes to a church that taught a doctrine different from those that an individual espoused.[275] Waldman writes, "When Madison began his career as a legislator, one of the first issues he focused on was religious freedom."[276] This is a reference to, among other things, Madison's key support for the Virginia Statute of Religious Freedom that was championed by Jefferson.[277] Madison once argued that "Whilst we assert for ourselves a freedom to...profess...the religion we believe to be of divine origin, we cannot deny an equal freedom to those whose minds have not yet yielded to the evidence which has convinced us."[278] Did Madison think that Christianity was

---

[273] Cheney, 39.

[274] David L. Holmes, *The Faiths of the Founding Fathers* (New York: Oxford University Press, 2006), 96.

[275] Thompson, Mary V. Thompson, *In the Hands of a Good Providence* (Charlottesville: University of Virginia Press, 2008). 156.

[276] Steven Waldman, *Founding Faith* (New York: Random House, 2008), 105.

[277] As mentioned in chapter two

[278] Jon Meacham, *American* Gospel, (New York: Random House, 2007), 85.

superior and inevitable, or was he just being charitable to a predominantly Christian audience?

Madison biographer Lynne Cheney theorizes that Madison wanted religious freedom partially because of "the misery he knew as a young man when he realized that Christian orthodoxy insisted on a supernatural explanation for (his) epilepsy."[279] The problem with this theory, though, is that Christian orthodoxy does not and did not demand a spiritual explanation for medical issues. Some Christians associate poor health with God's wrath, and one could argue that more people did so back then, but an intelligent and well-educated man like Madison would know that his "thorn in the flesh,"[280] as St. Paul so famously put it, was not necessarily a sign of God's displeasure.

Madison's view regarding freedom of religion was not code for a personal freedom from religion. Madison was a churchgoer who consorted with pastors—inviting them into his home—and he engaged in family prayers. He did not kneel during prayer on these occasions, and some people find that significant.[281] Was he emulating the behavior of his fellow Virginian and friend George Washington, or did Madison have bad knees? The historical record is not clear. Still, it is easy to imagine—but not prove—that Madison stood during prayer as a show of respect to God. His churchgoing, too, was probably more than familial appeasement. Madison's wife, Dolley, was a Quaker before she married him, so she was probably not the sole driving force in their attendance at Episcopal worship.

Madison once wrote in *The Federalist Papers*, which were a series of essays explaining and defending the Constitution, of the "finger of that Almighty hand which has been so frequently and signally extended to our relief in the critical stages of the revolution."[282] The quotation in and of itself does not prove that Madison was an evangelical, but it is definitely not compatible with pure Deism. This sort of language was rather common back then, though not ubiquitous.

---

[279] Cheney, 72.

[280] 2 Corinthians 12:7.

[281] It was unclear from this source how Madison handled prayers in church. Did he, like Washington, always stand while praying? It is a mystery. Holmes, 91.

[282] It was in Federalist Number 37. Meacham, 87-88.

It does not prove anything, but it does add to the religious tapestry one can construct of the fourth president. Of course, if Madison was really serious about his faith in this specific timeframe then it stands to reason that there would have been some kind of reference to God in the Constitution, which Madison is considered the father of. But there is no religious language to be found there.

In 1790 someone started a rumor that Madison had become a Methodist. Actually, he had been born in the Anglican Church, as mentioned before, but he had never gone through confirmation.[283] He seemed attracted to the Presbyterian Church in college, but he never joined it. Still, these influences were much stronger on him than Methodism ever was.

When Madison was living in the White House, he attended St. John's Church, which was located next to the Executive Mansion. While he was at home on his plantation, he and his family attended St. Thomas Church. Both of these were Episcopal Churches, so his hostility towards the idea of an established church should not be assumed to be part of a general hostility towards the Episcopal faith. Interestingly, though Madison was never confirmed, faith was important to the women in his family—his mother and his wife Dolley both went through Episcopal confirmation.[284]

Madison demonstrated a consistency of thought regarding church and state when he vetoed an 1811 bill from Congress that would have incorporated a branch of the Episcopal Church in Washington DC. Madison argued that this clearly violated the Constitution's first amendment—Congress was not supposed to pass laws establishing religion.[285] This was an echo of Virginia's Statute for Religious Freedom: The government should not be in the business of forcing people to support a religion.

Later in life Madison tended to avoid public correspondences about his specific religious beliefs. He brought ministers to his

---

[283] Broadwater, 5.

[284] Holmes, 94.

[285] James Madison, *A Compilation of the Messages and Papers of the Presidents,* Volume 1, Part 4, Editor James D. Richardson (FQ Books, 2010), Kindle. Location 555-564.

plantation, so that his mother could observe Communion, and Madison participated.[286] Despite the fact that Madison was not confirmed in the Anglican/Episcopal Church, in the words of Waldman, "Madison never seemed to lose his view that Christianity was, on some level, the superior religion." In fact in 1832, he referred to the Christian faith as "the best and purest religion."[287]

In contrast to the opinion of many modern writers, Bishop William Meade renders his verdict on Madison's faith with the words "favorable opinion of his religious belief."[288] One could argue that Madison started out with orthodox beliefs, drifted off the mark—especially during his close association with Jefferson—and drifted back towards orthodoxy the closer he got to actually meeting his Maker. This was the position of Bishop Meade, and though historian David L. Holmes did not come to the same conclusion, Holmes concedes "that development would be unsurprising" because "old age is often the time when people return 'home' by embracing the faith in which they were raised."[289]

As stated in chapter three, Meade has some credibility when he offers opinions on the faith of the Virginians because he does not claim that they all were Christians. He does not argue for Jefferson, nor does he try to claim James Monroe as a believer. Also, Meade knew people who knew these presidents, which does not make his sources perfect, but it does give him a perspective not shared by modern historians.

Madison did not feel the necessity to put his religion on display as much as his predecessors did. He did not need to invoke its unifying effects like Washington, nor did Madison speak on religion to deal with skeptics making accusations of atheism against him like Jefferson. Again as with Jefferson, Madison referenced God in an inaugural address[290] and championed religious freedom, but it was not as paramount for the fourth president to do these things.

---

[286] Broadwater, 5.

[287] Waldman, 99.

[288] Bishop William Meade, *Old Churches, Ministers, and Families of Virginia* (Philadelphia: J.B. Lippincott and Co., 2011), 16-22. Kindle.

[289] Holmes, 97.

[290] John Gabriel Hunt, *The Inaugural Addresses of the Presidents* (New York:

Given Madison's publicly stated affirmations of Christianity, the seriousness with which he took prayer, the faithfulness he had to his church, and the almost contemporary appraisal of Meade, a reasonable person might justifiably assume that Madison ended his life as an orthodox believer. While multiple historians disagree with this assessment, the fact that his orthodoxy is at least arguable is a distinction that puts him in contrast with the two men who held the presidency immediately before him.

Growing up, the earliest Virginia presidents faced a challenge not experienced by their counterparts in Massachusetts. The problem was described by Jefferson. As historian Edmund S. Morgan puts it, "In Jefferson's own view the education of young Virginians was unlikely to make anything but tyrants among them, especially those who spent their early years, as he did, on one of the great plantations." Morgan goes on to quote Jefferson, "The whole commerce between master and slave is a perpetual exercise of…the most unremitting despotism on the one part, and degrading submissions on the other." Jefferson noted that as children watched their fathers in this dynamic, they imitated the behaviors among themselves. It was Jefferson's belief that "The man must be a prodigy who can retain his morals undepraved by such circumstances."[291] Madison, like Washington and Jefferson before him, came from a slave owning family.

It would be easy to dismiss Madison and his fellow Virginia planters as men who must thus automatically be comfortable with slavery, but this was not the case. Madison demonstrated this with his opposition to a proposal raised in the Virginia Assembly. Virginia was having trouble enticing enough men into military service during the Revolutionary War, so someone suggested that each enlistee should be promised a slave. The measure was defeated, and Madison was a key part of the opposition. He argued that it would "be more consonant to the principles of liberty" to make soldiers of the slaves themselves."[292]

Gramercy Books, 2003), 42.
[291] Edmund S. Morgan, *American Slavery—American Freedom* (New York: W.W. Norton & Company, 1975), 375.
[292] Cheney, 94.

This was not going to happen, of course. Southern whites were terrified at the thought of armed African Americans—there would be too much of a possibility for retribution after all the years of cruelty—but Madison could not ignore the fact that this was a war about liberty. He felt that he had to live with a certain measure of hypocrisy as a slave owner supporting a struggle for liberty, but the man had reached his limit.

In Madison's Eighth Annual Message to Congress as president, he applauded the United States for being the first country to outlaw the overseas slave trade, and he admonished Congress to put more teeth into this fight.[293] One wants to give Madison credit for this, but there is a question that comes to mind. Was Madison at all motivated to keep more slaves from entering the country so his slaves would have more value if he wanted to sell them? Since Madison resisted the temptation of profiting through selling slaves to other, potentially cruel owners, his motives look pure on this topic. [294]

Madison knew that slavery was an "unfortunate stain" on slave owners and the nation as a whole.[295] But like so many of the other Founders, he did not know what to do about it for himself or the country. Legally, he did not have the power as president to order the end of slavery. Even Lincoln's great Emancipation Proclamation only ended slavery in most of the South;[296] slavery lived on in the North until the 13th Amendment was passed. In other words, slavery could only be ended by changing the Constitution, which Madison could not do unilaterally.

As Madison neared death, friends encouraged him to make provisions to free his slaves in his will. If he could not free all slaves, at least he could free his own, his friends argued. Unfortunately, the all-

---

[293] Madison, L 2464, 2531-2539.

[294] Kenneth O'Reilly, *Nixon's Piano* (New York: Free Press, 1995), 26-27.

[295] Ibid., 26-27.

[296] The exact description of which states had slavery ended by the Emancipation Proclamation would be the Rebel states that the Union had not yet re-taken by the time the Proclamation went into effect. For example, Tennessee was a Confederate state that had already been brought back under Union control, so Tennessee was already working on its own plan for ending slavery.

too-logical Madison saw the difficulties of such a proposition. Freeing his slaves upon his death would leave Dolley on an already indebted plantation with no labor force. Freeing them upon Dolley's death would put her in the same situation Martha Washington was in after her husband died: terrified that their slaves might hasten her departure from this life in order to speed up their departure from bondage.[297]

Another problem with freeing a large number of slaves at one time was that they were required to leave the state, but Madison knew they were unwelcome in the free states in the US, in Canada, and in Haiti. At least, Madison was convinced, there was a long-term solution to the re-settlement issue—the African colonization plan mentioned in chapter two. Though there were issues with the plan, and ultimately it would prove untenable, it allowed Madison to dream of better days ahead when America could shed itself of what he considered the "dreadful calamity" of slavery.[298] He actually spent many hours in retirement working fruitlessly on the particulars of this plan.[299]

There is an alternate version of the above story. Edward Coles, who was the secretary of and a friend to Madison, claimed that the fourth president left his slaves to his wife with the understanding that she would free them when she died. If this was their agreement then Dolley is responsible for failing to keep it.[300] Though there is no definitive proof of this story being true, it seems plausible: James could have assuaged his conscience, but the plan was discrete enough that it would not have left Dolley fearing for her life. She did not follow through because of the dire economic circumstances that she faced. The bottom line, though, is that James Madison had a number of slaves under his control, and he did not like slavery, but his slaves were not freed. The official documentation—his will—contained a request that Dolley would only sell slaves with their consent or as punishment for wrongdoing. For the most part, she honored this.[301]

---

[297] Cheney, 452.
[298] Ibid.
[299] O'Reilly, 28.
[300] Leibiger, n 254-255.
[301] Cheney, 455.

The leadership experiences of James Madison were almost quite different from what they turned out to be. He might have ended up as an officer in the Continental Army during the Revolution, except for one problem. He had trained with the Virginia militia, and he was pretty good with a rifle, but because he had some kind of medical condition that could well have been epilepsy, he pursued political science instead of the military arts.[302]

As he embarked on a career in politics, a leadership quality Madison possessed was an extraordinary ability to think on his feet. When delegates in the state of Virginia were voting on whether or not to approve the Constitution, the anti-federalists—meaning those who were against approval—were led by a potent trio. During the debate Patrick Henry, James Monroe, and George Mason took turns rising and objecting to different portions of the document, and frequently Madison spoke in reply, even as he battled health issues. One of the other delegates commented that Madison "came boldly forward and supported the Constitution with the soundest reason and most manly eloquence I ever heard." Others, too, raved about Madison's brilliance in the debates, including one of his opponents: James Monroe.[303]

Madison was a brilliant man who engaged in serious contemplation and research. When America was struggling under the Articles of Confederation government, Madison studied history books that Jefferson gave him to figure out a solution. Madison came to the conclusion that the great confederations of the past eventually fell apart because the bonds that held them together were not strong enough. This was what gave Madison the conviction that a stronger government was needed[304] and sustained him in the face of opposition from some of Virginia's leading politicians.[305] Madison's strength was not just in knowledge itself, but in the wisdom that does not always accompany it. It was the evidence of this wisdom which prompted France's ambassador to the United States, the chevalier de la Luzerne, to

---

[302] Cheney, 51.

[303] Ibid., 174-177.

[304] Ibid., 116-117.

[305] And as his opponents gathered against him, Washington stayed at Mount Vernon, away from the fight; and Jefferson was overseas.

describe Madison as "the man of the soundest judgment in Congress." Luzerne was not alone. One of Madison's fellow politicians from Virginia, Edmund Randolph once said, "He who had once partaken of the rich banquet of (Madison's) remarks did not fail to wish daily to sit within the reach of his conversation."[306]

As George Washington prepared to become the first president, he asked for Madison's help with the inaugural address. After the inauguration, Madison was picked to pen the reply from the House of Representatives. Upon hearing from this body, the first president decided a brief response was in order, so he asked for Madison's help again. Basically, Madison was writing speeches back and forth to himself, explaining how the branches of government were going to conduct their business.[307] He certainly did not have the high profile of Washington, but was anyone in the country providing more leadership at this point than James Madison?

Jefferson biographer Jon Meacham describes Madison as "an invaluable architect of Jefferson's own career."[308] Given Jefferson's undeniable successes, this is lofty praise indeed.

Part of Madison's giftedness as a leader was his ability to collaborate with great men, even when these men were quite different from one another. While in the Continental Congress, the young Virginian "had become firmly allied," according to one biographer, with the much older Pennsylvanian, Ben Franklin.[309] Madison was so close to George Washington that the first president relied on him for advice on all kinds of things, including "relations with Congress, etiquette, appointments, and policy."[310] Washington refused to support the political party system, but Madison worked with him effectively for several years. Alexander Hamilton would eventually become Madison's archenemy as the leader of the Federalist Party, but early on they worked together to set up the constitutional convention. Madison,

---

[306] Cheney, 56, 97.
[307] Ibid., 186-188.
[308] Jon Meacham, *Thomas Jefferson* (New York: Random House, 2012), 122.
[309] Cheney, 83.
[310] Stuart Leibiger, *Founding Friendship* (Charlottesville: University of Virginia Press, 2001), 109.

Hamilton, and Jon Jay then defended the work of that convention by co-authoring *The Federalist Papers*. Finally, of course, Madison and Jefferson were the leaders of the Democratic-Republicans.

Something that helped Madison fulfill the role of Great Collaborator was that he could form a genuine attachment to someone and even ideological differences would not necessarily interfere with personal loyalty. This was a perspective that Washington sometimes lacked,[311] Adams only displayed with Jefferson, and Quincy Adams would have been baffled by.

Madison's closest and most enduring collaboration was with Thomas Jefferson. Though Jefferson would loom larger in history, Madison had a few qualities that Jefferson lacked. Both men were brilliant. Madison biographer Lynne Cheney speculates that "each was probably the brightest person the other ever knew." Jefferson sometimes had ideas that "became untethered from reality, but Madison drew him back to solid earth." Also, Madison knew how to laugh at himself and tell the occasional self-deprecating story, behavior which was not Jefferson's style.[312]

Madison's personal loyalty was on display late in his life. In 1828 Madison was asked to share publicly his private correspondence with Washington. Madison declined because, he said, some of Washington's letters were "written in haste" and as a result contained "specks of inaccuracy which…might disappoint readers." Rather than even slightly tarnish the image of a friend who had died in the last century, Madison kept the letters private.[313] Such loyalty is an inspiring trait to see in a leader.

Harlow Giles Unger was a biographer of Madison's successor in the White House, so Unger is quite familiar with Madison, too. The historian was rather brutal in his assessment of the fourth president, saying, "Madison had been a superb political theoretician, but he was no leader." Unger accused Madison of having no policies of his own. As a result, the Father of the Constitution either maintained Jefferson's policies, regardless of whether or not they were still relevant, or

---

[311] Leibiger, 222.
[312] Cheney, 70-71.
[313] Leibiger, 225.

Madison allowed himself to be pushed around by Democratic-Republican leaders in Congress.[314]

Madison biographer Lynne Cheney portrays the fourth president as a strong leader who was outraged by British provocations and thus pushed Congress to prepare sufficiently for what would be the War of 1812.[315] But Monroe's biographer, Unger, has a different perception of things. According to Unger, Madison was guilty of not sufficiently rallying support for the war, despite years of outrageous behavior by the British. As a result, people from New England and New York referred to the conflict as "Mr. Madison's War," and considered him to be just a tool of the French,[316] which was hardly something many people would say about a strong leader.

When Madison served as secretary of state, the second most important office in the land, Unger describes him as merely Jefferson's puppet. But during Madison's service as president, Unger says that Monroe was really the "de facto president and commander in chief for nearly two years."[317]

Unger goes on to say that earlier, Madison had inadvertently insulted Monroe by offering his fellow Virginian the governorship of the Louisiana Territory after Monroe had already turned down the offer when Jefferson made it. As a result, according to Unger, "The incompetent Madison was left to totter in his rickety presidential chair."[318]

The impression of Madison as a weakling has early origins. His first Secretary of State, Robert Smith, frequently undermined Madison's agenda. When Madison finally decided to fire Smith, thus opening the door for James Monroe, Smith responded with an angry pamphlet. The bitter and biased Smith argued that Madison was really the incompetent one, not Smith himself.[319]

---

[314] Harlow Giles Unger, *The Last Founding Father* (Philadelphia: Da Capo, 2010), 207.
[315] Cheney, 372-378.
[316] Unger, 223-224.
[317] Ibid., 210, 259.
[318] Ibid., 208.
[319] Cheney, 368-369.

There are those who believe that Madison only agreed to the War of 1812 with great reluctance. This theory maintains that it was Congress that wanted to stand up to Great Britain's contemptuous behavior at sea and in the Old Northwest Territory. Lynne Cheney argues that Madison's reluctance was not driven by timidity, but by Madison's very reasonable concern that the country should be ready for war before entering into it.[320]

According to the Constitution, Congress is the body entrusted to declare war. When they did that with Britain in 1812, Madison issued a proclamation that certainly seems stirring enough. It includes a call for vigilance and zealousness on the part of Americans, and it also makes appeals to patriotism and prayer.[321] Whatever Madison's attitude had been about the war, the man could write a good speech.

James Madison was instrumental in crafting the Constitution, he skillfully defended it as the nation debated whether or not to accept it, and he helped implement it in the earliest days of the United States. He influenced Washington and Jefferson for the better, and Madison helped pave the way for James Monroe to succeed him. Madison saw the country through its second war with the most powerful nation in the world, and while the United States did not win, at least it did not lose. Madison was not the most forceful leader in the nation's history, but it is easy to argue that he was a successful one.

His record was not as good in the area of slavery. Madison was genuinely troubled by the institution, but other than fighting the idea of providing slaves for recruits, Madison really did nothing praiseworthy here.

In the area of faith, Madison's portrait is the grayest so far. He might have had orthodox Christian beliefs at the end of his life. Even if he did not, he seems more sympathetic to the traditional practice of Christianity than Adams or Jefferson, and Madison definitely saw religion as a beneficial institution.

---

[320] Cheney, 377.
[321] Madison, L 1098-1107.

CHAPTER 7

#5 JAMES MONROE

James Monroe deserves more attention than he gets, historically speaking. The Virginian fought with distinction in the Revolutionary War, getting wounded in the process. During the War of 1812, he served in not one but two Cabinet positions. He won seventy percent of the popular vote in his first victory then took every electoral vote but one in his re-election bid. Despite how impressive these achievements are, though, they do not answer the questions posed in this book. Monroe's military bravery does not provide insight into his faith. His background as a Virginia planter and politician suggests some things about his outlook on slavery, but it does describe the whole story. His election success indicates his popularity, but this is hardly the only measure of a politician's leadership. For insight into these things, we have to look deeper.

Monroe is generally portrayed as uninterested in religion. In fact, in a survey of three books about the faith of the Founders only one devotes a chapter to Monroe.[322] Of course, the other two authors might have felt that Monroe was only peripherally a Founding Father, so the omissions of Monroe do not exactly settle the debate.

---

[322] Holmes' book gives Monroe a thorough treatment; the books by Waldman and Mapp do not. David L. Holmes, *The Faiths of the Founding Fathers* (New York: Oxford University Press, 2006); Steven Waldman, *Founding Faith* (New York: Random House, 2008); Alf J. Mapp, Jr., Alf J. *The Faith of our Fathers* (New York: Fall River Press, 2006).

While Monroe was indifferent to the faith—maybe—he was at least exposed to it. Monroe was born in Westmoreland County, Virginia, only four miles from the birthplace of George Washington. In fact, Monroe's childhood school had been attended previously by Washington and Madison. Monroe was joined there by future Supreme Court Chief Justice John Marshall,[323] and they were all taught by an Anglican clergyman. The teacher/priest educated his pupils regarding the Bible along with math, history, Latin and French. In Monroe's case, he only spent about twelve weeks a year attending classes because of his responsibilities during the harvesting and planting that took place on his family's property.

When Monroe attended William and Mary, it was in many ways an Anglican college. Most of the members of the faculty were members of the local Anglican congregation, and Monroe was required to attend morning and evening prayer services, as well as Sunday worship at the local church.[324] The college had been founded with the idea of training pastors, though it quickly drifted from its roots into a more secularized experience for its students.[325]

Monroe, like Madison, attended St. John's Episcopal Church in Washington D.C. when president, but other than that he did not leave much of a religious footprint while in the Oval Office. As David L. Holmes puts it, "Even those who have written books on the religion of the American presidents have found little to say when they have reached the religion of the fifth president of the United States." Holmes characterizes Monroe's public utterances about faith as numbering "remarkably little." Monroe destroyed the private letters he shared with his wife, so any insight into his religiosity from that source is lost. [326]

The fifth president did have at least a season of warm religious sentiment. When Monroe was stationed in Valley Forge along with his fellow Continentals during the American Revolution, he wrote a letter

---

[323]Robert Pierce Forbes, *The Missouri Compromise and its Aftermath* (Chapel Hill: University of North Carolina Press, 2007). Kindle. Location 356.
[324] Holmes, 99.
[325] Harlow Giles Unger, *The Last Founding Father* (Philadelphia: Da Capo Press, 2009), 14.
[326] Holmes, 100-101.

to a gravely ill friend who was Catholic. Monroe wrote, "'Tis the summit of Christian fortitude...to prevail over the views of this transitory life, and to turn the mind on the more lasting happiness to come."[327]

Perhaps Monroe did not retain his Christian zeal, if indeed that is what it was, but his life was not as devoid of religion as some historians have indicated. A few months before Thomas Jefferson's wife died, Monroe sent a letter that said Monroe was praying that "it may please heaven to restore" Martha Jefferson.[328] This does not make Monroe an evangelical, but it does seem to contradict the argument that he was a Deist. Of course, one could argue that Monroe was simply borrowing some comforting language from a faith he and Jefferson was raised in, even if they no longer believed in it.

Monroe was certainly not an abolitionist, but a religious sensibility is seen in some of his thoughts on the subject. As Monroe biographer Harlow Giles Unger puts it, "Monroe had no strong objections to slavery," but the Virginian did acknowledge that, "The God who made us, made the black people, and they ought not be treated with barbarity."[329]

For a man who was supposed to be irreligious, Monroe had some interesting things to say about his prayer life. In his second Inaugural Address, the fifth president said, "The liberty, prosperity, and happiness of our country will always be the object of my most fervent prayers to the Supreme Author of All Good."[330] In 1824 Monroe gave his last presidential address to Congress, and in his message he discussed the good fortune of the United States. He said, "That these blessings may be preserved and perpetuated will be the object of my fervent and unceasing prayers to the Supreme Ruler of the Universe."[331]

---

[327] Holmes, 101-102.

[328] Unger, 42; Jon Meacham *Thomas Jefferson* (New York: Random House, 2012), 145.

[329] Unger, 306.

[330] William J. Federer, *America's God and Country: Encyclopedia of Quotations* (St. Louis: Amerisearch, 2000), 452.

[331] Unger, 330-331.

There was a common religious theme to Monroe's speeches at the beginning of both presidential terms. During his First Inaugural Address, he spoke approvingly of our freedom of worship. In the conclusion of his second one, he spoke of his "firm reliance on the protection of Almighty God."[332]

Some reference to God or Providence was common in political speeches, as evidenced by the fact that all of Monroe's presidential predecessors included such remarks in their inaugural addresses.[333] Acknowledging that, would it occur to an irreligious man to speak of "unceasing prayers?" Possibly it would, but such religious language should not be automatically dismissed, just because it was used elsewhere by others.

Maybe these were simply public platitudes. But how many times does the fifth president have to talk about prayer before the scales tip, and it becomes the responsibility of the skeptic to prove Monroe's lack of faith?

Perhaps Monroe simply looks less religious than his fellow Founders from Virginia because Washington was an advocate of religion during the war, and Jefferson and Madison were such proponents of religious freedom, that there is more material in the historical record regarding these three men in general.

Be that as it may, the best an evangelical might be able to argue for Monroe is that he was a man of prayer. The lack of references to Christ by Monroe other than his sentiments as a young man in the war, make it difficult to argue that he was a Christian. One is left without a Madisonian tribute to Christianity, a record of service in his church comparable to Washington's, or a positive judgment from the Episcopal Bishop Meade. Thus, one could be left to argue that the Christian religion might have played a role in Monroe's presidency even if it might not have played a major role in his heart.

---

[332] James Monroe, *A Compilation of the Messages and Papers of the Presidents,* Volume 2, Part 1, Editor James D. Richardson (FQ Books, 2006), Kindle. Location 65-73, 2088.
[333] Gabriel Hunt, *The Inaugural Addresses of the Presidents* (New York: Gramercy Books, 2003). 4, 9, 19, 42.

There were periods where the nation's politicians avoided talk of slavery, but for a southerner like James Monroe, its reality was never far from his mind. The conversion of many southern plantations from tobacco production to cotton had a major impact on the institution of slavery, as alluded to in chapter two. Tobacco farming required a more complicated sequence of steps, so not just anyone could do it. Historian Harlow Giles Unger theorizes that there were tobacco plantations where as many as two-thirds of the slaves generally performed little to no substantive work. Cotton farming did not require the same level of skill. Children and the elderly could be compelled to participate now. Where previously part of the white population had resented slaves who were skilled laborers and thus rivals for jobs, now these same whites envisioned buying a small section of land and working on it with slaves of their own. With a higher percentage of slaves now able to be productive in the fields, they were suddenly much more affordable.[334]

Now that children and the elderly were increasingly being forced into the fields, the paternalistic vision of ownership was harder to maintain. Discipline intensified; resentment brewed. Slave rebellions, and the threat thereof, became an increasing reality that Monroe dealt with as Governor of Virginia.[335] In such a changing dynamic, it is not surprising that people like Monroe believed that shipping slaves off to Africa or someplace else was a logical way to avoid bloodshed on both sides.

Smith Thompson, first mentioned in chapter two, played a pivotal role as secretary of the navy in Monroe's plan to end slavery and send the slaves to Africa. Obviously a navy would be needed to move such a large group of people. Monroe and Thompson were both members of the American Colonization Society, and they wanted their plan to work. They saw the threat to sectional harmony, the threat of deadly slave revolts, and the negative moral impact on slave owners. But they also recognized that the system itself was unfair, especially in a land that prided itself on liberty.[336]

---

[334] Unger, 140-141.
[335] Ibid.
[336] Forbes, L 549-575.

Ultimately, the colonization plan failed for several reasons. Owners did not want to part with their slaves. There were never sufficient funds to pay off owners, or haul former slaves to Africa. Many former slaves did not trust white shippers, which makes sense given the history involved. Even if trust had not been an issue, for many former slaves who were born and raised in America, Africa was a strange and dangerous place; it did not represent home.

Monroe's conscience was soothed somewhat by a rationalization he shared with many other Americans: it was not their fault that slavery existed here. He blamed the British for foisting the institution on the colonists almost from the beginning. Monroe also rationalized that state governments were powerless to end the institution in such a way as to maintain peace with slaves who might well want revenge for the injustices they endured.[337]

When he was a member of the Articles of Confederation Congress, Monroe proposed that qualified territories be allowed full and equal admittance into the Union. As Monroe saw it, equality for the new states meant that slavery would be legal there.[338] Fortunately, when the new states in the Old Northwest territory were admitted, slavery was not allowed. Monroe was on the wrong side of history here.

Any additional geographical growth threatened to produce a new chapter in the arguments between pro-slavery forces and abolitionists. One might expect that a southerner and plantation owner would want to see the growth of slavery, but Monroe was more moderate than that. He was actually reluctant to endorse such growth, specifically into Florida and Texas, because of the controversy over slavery. Florida was acquired during Monroe's administration, but he was conflicted about the problem.[339]

The overseas slave trade would be outlawed on January 1, 1808, and many Americans assumed that after that had happened, slavery would die out. Indeed, it was already dying in the North. Legislatures in

---

[337] Unger, 147.
[338] Ibid., 60.
[339] Charles N. Edel, *Nation Builder* (Cambridge, MA: Harvard University Press, 2014), 156.

several states were putting extinction dates on the institution, and many of these states were seeing it disappear before their deadlines.[340]

In the South, however, the slave population continued to grow, and it multiplied at a faster rate than the white population,[341] making the problem harder to fix. It was not just that slaves were reproducing, there were many smugglers who ignored the ban on the slave trade. There was money to be made and not much of a social stigma for northerners or southerners involved in the wretched practice.[342]

By 1819, Virginia had almost 500,000 slaves, but there was not nearly enough work to keep them occupied.[343] Freeing at least a portion of them might sound like simple logic to twenty-first century thinkers, but slaves had value. Overextended planters were not going to shed capital without compensation, especially given the legal restrictions on manumission that existed in Virginia and elsewhere in the South. The more logical solution to the planters was to sell their surplus slaves to cotton growers out of state.

As the situation with Missouri was being debated, Monroe ordered his Cabinet to stay out of it, and he told them to keep him out of it, too. This hardly looks like leadership: the president went to great lengths to stay on the sidelines during the most important domestic debate facing the country. But the Constitution said that qualified territories were to be admitted as states without special restrictions or limits, and Congress was supposed to oversee this process.[344] Monroe could argue with no small amount of credibility that Missouri was none of his business. Given that he was a slave owning southerner, his decision to not advocate for the South actually says something positive about his character.

James Monroe profited from the forced labor of men, women, and children, but it was the culture into which he was born. He was troubled by it, though in fairness to the truth, much of his concern centered on the fear of rebellion from people who were pushed too far.

---

[340] Forbes, L 100.
[341] Sam W. Haynes *James K. Polk* (New York: Pearson Longman, 2006), 105.
[342] Forbes, L 669-677.
[343] Ibid., L 126-127.
[344] Unger, 305-306.

He resisted the impulse to push for its expansion, and he dreamed and schemed of ways to be rid of it. Acknowledging all of this, it must be noted that he could probably have done more. In the end, he has at best a mixed record on this issue. It would be easy to argue that even calling his record "mixed" is too charitable.

Great leaders are typically people with foresight, and Monroe had that. As a delegate of the Articles of Confederation government, Monroe proposed allowing western territories to be granted statehood on equal footing with the original thirteen. This was voted down, which was good because, as mentioned above, Monroe's plan included the allowance of slavery. But there were those who thought the new states should be of lesser status than the originals, so in this regard, Monroe had a stronger vision of liberty (at least for white westerners) than some did.[345]

Monroe's vision was not always so clear, however. When the country began to consider discarding the Articles of Confederation in favor of the Constitution, Monroe originally was in favor of it, swayed by Washington and Madison. But Monroe allowed himself to be turned against the Constitution by Patrick Henry, who was afraid that personal liberty might be in jeopardy.[346] Obviously, Monroe made his peace with the new government and eventually became president, but modern political opponents might characterize his position(s) here as a flip-flop.

Monroe's predecessor, James Madison, might have been great at collaborating, but the fourth president's relationship with Monroe was not always so harmonious. Long before Madison offended Monroe by offering him the governorship of the Louisiana Territory,[347] the two men ran against each other for a seat in the first House of Representatives. As mentioned, Monroe was against the new

---

[345] Unger, 68-69.
[346] Ibid., 78-79.
[347] Monroe had greater ambitions, and he felt this offer was beneath him. Or, one could argue that the position in Louisiana was an effort to move Monroe far away from Washington, DC. The generous-sounding offer might have been designed to isolate Monroe, politically and geographically. Unger, 192.

Constitution, and he was part of a movement that hoped to win a majority in the new federal government in order to pass legislation that would cripple it. It says something about both men's character that they maintained their friendship with each other, even though they were opponents in the race with different political philosophies. They traveled together and shared accommodations while on the campaign trail. It also says something about Monroe's character that he eventually saw the virtues in this new government, and eventually became a key figure in it, despite losing that initial race to Madison.[348]

Monroe gained quite a bit of leadership experience over the years, but he paid a heavy price for it. He was chosen for a seat in the United States Senate, but that only happened after losing the House race to Madison. Monroe later served as the Minister (Ambassador) to France under George Washington, but Monroe was relieved of his duties and humiliated in the process by Washington's last secretary of state, Timothy Pickering. Pickering was a highly partisan Federalist, and he was pro-Britain in that country's dispute with France, which was favored by Democratic-Republicans like Monroe.[349]

Monroe did not fear controversy. Initially, he was intimidated when he began his term in the Senate—he was a young man surrounded by a cast that included several older men who could legitimately claim the status of Founding Fathers. Monroe found his voice when he attacked and sought to end the Senate's secrecy rules, which forbade the public from watching their proceedings. Monroe's proposal was shot down, but the incident showed that he was willing to take a risky and provocative stand for what he considered to be a righteous cause.[350]

While Jefferson gets credit for doubling the size of the country with the Louisiana Purchase, it should be noted that Monroe was one of the diplomats who helped broker the deal. Monroe's team was supposed to try to get New Orleans, but they ended up with so much more. Great leaders exceed expectations.

---

[348] Unger, 82-83.
[349] Ibid., 124-135.
[350] Ibid., 87-88.

As historian Robert Forbes points out, Monroe might have been better able to see the big picture than his two immediate predecessors because of Monroe's life experience. Monroe had served as a diplomat in both France and Britain, so over time he had a balanced view of our relations in Europe. Also, Monroe married a northern woman, which helped him see beyond a sectional bias.[351] Jefferson married a fellow southerner, and while Jefferson served happily in France as a diplomat, his experiences in Britain were negative. Madison married a northern woman, but he never visited Europe at all. Thus, Monroe naturally acquired a more national and global perspective than Jefferson or Madison.

Monroe returned to Washington from Europe after a final tenure of valuable, overseas diplomatic service. This time it was near the end of Jefferson's second term as president. Monroe met with his good friends, Jefferson and Madison, hoping to know what role he could fill in an expected Madison administration. For whatever combination of reasons, Jefferson and Madison avoided the subject. Theories have been offered regarding why this discussion did not take place, but concrete facts are lacking and off point here.[352]

What is relevant to this book is that Monroe felt unappreciated and chose to let it hurt his feelings. Several of his fellow Virginians expressed their support for the idea of Monroe being president instead of Madison. Briefly put, the ongoing tensions between Britain and France were creating problems for the United States. The efforts of Jefferson and Madison to apply economic pressure on those countries backfired, temporarily hurting both northern industries and southern agricultural interests. Jefferson was almost as highly esteemed as Washington had been, making Virginians reluctant to blame him. Besides, Jefferson was not running for a third term. Thus, his secretary of state, Madison, became the target for popular frustration. Virginians wanted an alternative to Madison, and Monroe decided to give them one.[353]

---

[351] Forbes, L 390-391.
[352] Unger, 197-199; Forbes, L 433.
[353] Unger, 196-197.

Just as with the Constitution, though, Monroe again changed his mind. Was it a humbleness of spirit, or a lack of resolution? One could argue either way, but Monroe gave up his opposition, and it was a two-step process. First, in an unusual display on Jefferson's part, he apologized for hurting Monroe's feelings.[354] Second, and due in no small part to Jefferson's endorsement, Madison won what amounted to a political primary in Virginia by a convincing margin over Monroe. After this, Monroe withdrew from the race, and Madison became the next president. Because Monroe did not actively campaign on his own behalf—men back then "stood" for president; they did not "run" for the office in the modern sense of asking for votes—or publicly criticize Madison, it was easy for the two men to move past an awkward patch in their relationship yet again.[355]

A sign of a good leader is the ability to learn from the right role models. In 1807 Chief Justice of the Supreme Court, and Monroe's childhood friend, John Marshall published a five-volume biography of Marshall's friend and Monroe's hero, George Washington. Monroe read the work and was inspired. The biography influenced the course of Monroe's life moving forward.[356]

In 1808, Monroe decided that his time in service to his country had come to an end. He could have practiced law, but he emulated George Washington instead. Monroe decided to make his plantation truly profitable over the long term by rotating a variety of crops, like George Washington did. And just as it was with Washington, some of Monroe's neighbors were openly cynical about turning away from tobacco. Monroe knew, though, that tobacco would wear out the land.[357]

Before long, Monroe was pulled back into politics, serving as Madison's secretary of state for many years. As stated in the last chapter, the office of secretary of state was second only to the presidency in this era, but Monroe might have taken the office to a new level. He also briefly held the position of secretary of war. Thanks to

---

[354] It was unusual in that by its very nature, an apology represents an acknowledgement of wrong doing.

[355] Unger, 199-201.

[356] Ibid., 258.

[357] Ibid., 202.

Monroe's military experience during the Revolution, his insight was especially useful to the president during the War of 1812. Monroe became, in the words of his biographer Harlow Giles Unger, "de facto president and commander in chief for nearly two years,"[358] which was a bit of an overstatement, but it does indicate a powerful presence.

When Monroe officially became president, he offered a bold vision for the country. He wanted to promote unity, which meant reaching out to Federalists. He did not go so far as to give them Cabinet offices, but he did want people to look past party and sectional differences to a degree more than Jefferson and Madison had. This helped drive Monroe's choice of John Quincy Adams as secretary of state. The Federalist-turned-Democratic-Republican and New England native was a well-qualified choice, but not the type made by Monroe's immediate predecessors.[359] Monroe, like his five predecessors in office, thought that he should not be seen as the leader of a party while president. Monroe wanted to be above that.[360]

He also wanted to see growth in national defense, travel, manufacturing, and agriculture.[361] And, as mentioned above, he wanted to end slavery while making sure that the threat of racial tension was removed.[362] All of this was a little too ambitious—he basically called for an improvement of everything.

When Monroe was elected to his first term as president in 1816, he decided that once again he would follow in the first president's footsteps. Monroe took a tour of the nation, as Washington had early in his own first term. Thousands of citizens turned out as Monroe went from city to city. Many old veterans from the Revolution were on hand to see one of their own.[363] Monroe was able to appeal to the patriotism of the people who had so recently survived a second struggle with Britain in the War of 1812.

---

[358] Unger, 227, 232, 259.

[359] Forbes, L 456-486.

[360] Ralph Ketcham, *Presidents above Party* (Chapel Hill: University of North Carolina Press, 1984), xi; Unger, 325.

[361] Unger, 263.

[362] Forbes, L 303.

[363] Unger, 268-269.

According to historian Charles N. Edel, "Monroe…was not worried about placing strong personalities and bright people around him. He attempted to make executive decisions by the consensus of his Cabinet."[364] Edel sees Monroe as a self-confident leader with "a light touch."[365] Edel also believes Monroe was a pragmatic leader who nevertheless was a passionate supporter of republican revolutions against monarchies.[366]

Yet, Henry Clay, probably the most significant politician of the early to mid 1800s to not become president, commented to John Quincy Adams on the weakness of Monroe's presidency relative to the strength of Congress.[367]

Another argument regarding Monroe's lack of strength as a leader was his choice to keep himself and his Cabinet out of the debate over slavery in Missouri. It might have been constitutionally justifiable, as mentioned above, but it was an opportunity to at least speak decisively on a critically important issue. Monroe stayed silent.

What Monroe considered to be one of the greatest accomplishments during his administration actually turned out to be the one thing that ultimately undermined him. Like Washington, Adams, and Jefferson before him, Monroe considered the two-party system to be a bad thing for America. It was during Monroe's tenure as president that the Federalists died out as a national party. Monroe wrote to Madison about the wonderful new age that had arrived. But without a natural foil, the members of Monroe's Cabinet had nothing more important than their own ambitions to guide them. The absence of an opposition party granted them the luxury of not seeking unity for the good of the whole. There were no significant issues that readily separated them. Thus, for example, Secretary of the Treasury William Crawford lied to Monroe about the government's finances in a scheme to embarrass Secretary of War John Calhoun's political future. Monroe

---

[364] Edel, 118.
[365] Charles N. Edel, interview with author, April 7, 2015.
[366] Edel, 176.
[367] Norma Lois Peterson *The Presidencies of William Henry Harrison & John Tyler* (Lawrence: University of Kansas Press, 1989), 8.

tried to stay above such controversies, which made him seem not so much superior as irrelevant in his second term.[368]

One way to assess leaders from the past is to consider how their contemporaries saw them. It is significant that Washington got every vote from the Electoral College both times he stood for the presidency. It is also worth noting, therefore, that when Monroe stood for re-election only one elector voted for someone else. There were three of the 235 electors who abstained, and the Federalist Party had collapsed, so there was no organized, national opposition, but 231 out of 235 is a pretty resounding endorsement of Monroe's leadership. As far as the nation as a whole was concerned, James Monroe was a good leader.

Monroe's leadership on slavery was another matter. He seems to have genuinely wished that the institution would go away, and he tried to work with a creative solution to the problem. But sometimes leaders need to do more than wish and try.

When it comes to the topic of faith, Monroe gave little for historians to work with, which is in itself significant. Monroe might have been a man of prayer—he definitely talked about it some—or he might have been a good politicians playing to the crowd. If his faith did not matter enough to him to send a clearer message then, one could argue his faith did not matter much to him.

---

[368] Unger, 309-311.

CHAPTER 8

#6 JOHN QUINCY ADAMS

An otherwise obscure Federalist named Harrison Otis once wrote regarding John Adams and John Quincy Adams that they exhibited "a combination of talents and good moral character with passions and prejudices calculated to defeat their own objects and embarrass their friends."[369] That might be as apt a description as any for the only two of the first seven presidents who failed to get reelected.

Is there any president who had a larger number of significant role models in his life than John Quincy Adams? Author Charles N. Edel points out that Adams spent time with Ben Franklin and Thomas Jefferson as a child then worked as a diplomat for Washington, John Adams, and Madison before becoming the secretary of state for James Monroe. And according to Edel, the younger Adams gave as well as he got. Adams's views impacted Washington's Farewell Address, Monroe's famous Latin American Doctrine, and Lincoln's Emancipation Proclamation.[370] That is not bad for a one-term president who did not even win the popular vote for the four years he served.

It is not easy growing up in the shadow of a great father. This was certainly not a burden carried by, for example, Washington or Monroe, whose fathers died when both future presidents were still young. But the younger Adams had big shoes to fill, and though his

---

[369] John F. Kennedy, *Profiles in Courage* (New York: Harper & Row, 1956), 32.
[370] Charles N. Edel, *Nation Builder* (Cambridge MA: Harvard University Press, 2014), 6.

father created opportunities for him, the elder Adams did nothing to make things easy.

In fact, John Adams did just the opposite.

The elder Adams once told his son, "You come into life with advantages which will disgrace you if your success is mediocre." The second president went on to say, "If you do not rise to the head of your profession, (and even) your country, it will be owing to your own laziness, slovenliness, and obstinacy."[371] Needless to say, that was quite a bit of pressure on a preteen.

The younger Adams worked hard to make his parents proud, and they greatly impacted his views on faith, slavery and leadership.

John Quincy Adams definitely had a strong religious side. Going to church twice on a Sunday was not unusual for him.[372] Of course, it was typical behavior for many people back then. When visiting cities, George Washington and John Adams often found themselves attending churches twice on Sundays. Both father and son Adams liked to visit different denominations when traveling, and they would take extensive notes of the proceedings.[373]

Like many people throughout the ages, Adams found solace in his faith when circumstances seemed overwhelming. The sixth president faced three grave trials. First, his one term in office came to a disappointing end when he followed in his father's footsteps and failed to get re-elected as president in 1828. Adams' next problem involved one of his sons. The sixth president pursued his parental duties the way his parents did: he heaped a mountain-load of expectations on his oldest son and hoped for the best. By April 1829, a month after Adams left office, his son, George Washington Adams, could not deal with such unrelenting expectations, especially in light of his professional and personal failings—he was a debt-ridden failure as a lawyer, and despite being married he had gotten a servant pregnant. Quincy Adams' son killed himself.[374] The third trial faced by John Quincy Adams was when his wife, Louisa, became seriously ill following the suicide.

---

[371] Ellis, Joseph J., *First Family* (New York: Vintage Books, 2010), 92.
[372] Edel, 204.
[373] Charles N. Edel, interview with author, April 7, 2015.

In response to all of this, John Quincy read to her from the Bible, cried a lot, and asked God for guidance and mercy.[375]

Faith also helped to color Adams' attitude towards slavery. He believed that abolishing the institution was the duty of true Christians, and doing so was necessary for the country to fulfill its religious destiny.[376]

Adams' attention to Scripture was not a sporadic thing; he read one or two chapters a day throughout his life. Frequently, he included quotations from the Bible in letters and even in his diary. But while he saw it as more than just a book of morals or classical literature, he also refused to be drawn into, as he put it, "metaphysical subtleties."[377]

One such foray into metaphysics, as far as Adams was concerned, was the nature of Jesus of Nazareth. Rather than accepting the traditional, orthodox Christian view of Jesus as Divine Redeemer, Adams believed like his father that the carpenter's son was simply a man. John Quincy Adams did not espouse a belief in the Trinity.

Historian Jon Meacham is hardly guilty of reading too much Christianity into the Founders' lives—for example, he does not believe that Washington was a Christian—but Meacham refers to Adams as a "thoughtful Christian."[378] Adams recorded in his diary on July 21, 1833 that he wanted to spend the day in, as he described it, "religious meditation." His method of meditating that day was to read a book on religion that "any sincere Christian" should read multiple times.[379] Comments like this certainly might support Meacham's contention that Adams was a Christian and a deep thinker.

According to biographer Charles N. Edel, "It might be more accurate to say that both Adams were searchers. They visited various churches when they were in cities and took extensive notes on what

---

[374] Edel, 255.

[375] Edel, 255.

[376] Ibid., 280, 284-285.

[377] Ibid., 23, 113, 243.

[378] Which meant Meacham sees Quincy Adams as a Christian who was a deep thinker. Jon Meacham, *American Gospel* (New York: Random House, 2007), 78, 126.

[379] The work in question was a book of sermons by a preacher referred to only as "Saurin." Charles Francis Adams, Editor, *Memoirs of John Quincy Adams,* Kindle. Location. 6.

they observed." But when asked if such pursuits demonstrated theological or intellectual curiosity, Edel concedes that the answer is "Probably both."[380]

Of course, the foremost authority on the faith of John Quincy Adams is Adams himself. He wrote in his diary on April 4, 1820, "All the facts related of the life and death of Jesus may be disbelieved, and his precepts as a teacher of morals and religion be adopted" Adams went on to say that basically the narrative portions of both Old and New Testaments were works of fiction.[381]

This rejection of the Bible as authoritative was not a one-time opinion for Adams. Two months later, Adams wrote, "The idea that the execution as a malefactor of one human being should redeem the whole human race from a curse"…sets "all the reasoning faculties at defiance."[382] On July 8, 1833, Adams again expresses his frustration with a literal reading of the Bible. Focusing on the Old Testament, Adams finds miracles to be occurring too commonly, seemingly horrible things justified by the biblical writers as God's will, and behavior that strikes Adams as benign is condemned with the same justification.[383]

While the sixth president may have embraced Unitarianism, his wife most assuredly did not. Louisa Adams did not object to going to a Unitarian Church, but she did believe that all of the preachers of that sect were "enveloped in a cloud of mist."[384]

As a woman of her time, she did not have the full extent of educational opportunities afforded to intellectually promising and well-connected young men, and she was conscious of what she was lacking. Louisa Adams writes in her diary, "Mine is a weak and humble mind; possessing little knowledge and bigoted to no particular decree." But she raised an interesting question for those like her husband who denied

[380] Edel, interview April 7, 2015.
[381] John Quincy Adams, *Diary of John Quincy Adams*, April 4, 1820. masshist.org, Accessed 11/27/2015.
[382] John Quincy Adams, June, 18, 1820.
[383] Charles Francis Adams, L 7-8.
[384] She expressed such sentiments in her diary in February 1821. Judith S. Graham, et al, *The Adams Papers* (Cambridge, MA: Belknap Press, 2013), 562.

the deity of Christ. If Jesus "is merely mortal why were the inspired apostles not equally great?" She pointed out that they, too, were filled with the Holy Spirit, they performed miracles, they were friends of Jesus, and taught by Him, so why did they not have equal status?[385]

Mrs. Adams has an intriguing point. One can dispute the miraculous claims regarding the disciples and Jesus, but that still does not answer her main question. If Jesus was just a man, why did He have a status that was so much greater than his followers? He was the founder of the movement, but if He was just a man then would he really be worth any more adoration than Peter or Paul?

She wrote in her diary of a Unitarian minister who visited her husband in July 1839 that he "conversed very freely with Mr. Adams upon creeds, of course condemning all but their own."[386] In addition to simply being an interesting characterization of her husband, the passage is noteworthy for its acknowledgement that the male Adams shared the Unitarian views of his guest.

Unlike southerners such as Washington who needed to have an epiphany about slavery, Adams was consistently against it. As early as 1804, while serving as a senator, Adams called slavery "an offense against the laws of nature and God."[387] By the time Adams joined Monroe's Cabinet in early 1817, the New Englander was, in the words of Monroe biographer Harlow Giles Unger, "a fervent proponent of emancipation."[388]

Adams was not a man who made or kept friends easily, but he thought he had one in John C. Calhoun. They were both nationalists and members of Monroe's small Cabinet. They would have a falling out in later years around the time that Calhoun went from being Adams' vice president to serving the same role in Andrew Jackson's administration.[389] Back when they were friends, Adams was shocked to

---

[385] The diary entry was for July 12, 1839. Graham, 737-738.

[386] Graham, 735.

[387] Edel, 250.

[388] Harlow Giles Unger, *The Last Founding Father* (Philadelphia: De Capo Press, 2010), 305.

[389] Calhoun is the only man in American history to be vice president for two different

hear Calhoun talk about the positive side of slavery.[390] It amazed Adams that an intelligent person thought slavery was a good thing.

Historian Kenneth O'Reilly quotes Adams as saying, "Slavery in a moral sense is an evil, but as connected with commerce it has its uses." O'Reilly thus argues, "Business rated higher than morality, so he left slavery alone." He concedes that Adams earned "a place in abolitionist lore," but only after leaving the presidency.[391] While it is true that Adams became more outspoken about slavery later in life, O'Reilly sells the sixth president short. Obviously, there were economic benefits to slavery, or it would not have been so hard to eradicate. Acknowledging that reality just points to Adams' honesty, not necessarily to an indifference regarding slavery.

One can get a sense of Adams' attitude towards the institution from a remark he made to an Illinois senator, Ninian Edwards, before the Election of 1824, stating that Adams only wanted Texas and Florida admitted into the Union as new states if slavery was forbidden there. It was a noteworthy position from such a committed nationalist.[392]

Unfortunately, as Adams saw it, there was no way to get slavery out of the states where it was already legal. He felt that the writers of the Constitution made "a dishonorable compromise with slavery" by which they were all now bound.[393]

Adams believed that pushing too hard for abolition in the Louisiana Territory might put the entire Union at risk. He also believed at least as early as 1820 that the issue of slavery would eventually split the country anyway with a crushing war that would exterminate the institution. Though much destruction would come from such fighting, Adams wrote, "As God shall judge me, I dare not say that it is not to be desired." That said, Adams believed that the nation needed to grow powerful enough that other nations would not try to take it over when America finally fought itself to be rid of slavery.[394]

---

men.
[390] Edel, 249.
[391] Kenneth O'Reilly, *Nixon's Piano* (New York: Free Press, 1995), 31.
[392] Edel, 155.
[393] Ibid., 157.
[394] Edel, 158-159, 250. Time did not diminish the threat that slavery presented to the

Interestingly, when Adams was elected president, he might have lacked a majority, even a plurality, but he did have the enthusiastic approval of African Americans in the nation's capital. They celebrated loudly when Adams' selection was announced.[395] Whatever they knew of his personal views, it makes sense that African Americans believed they were better off with a non-slave owning New Englander than with another plantation owning president.

Despite Adams' personal hatred of slavery, he did not advocate the end of it during his presidency. He was accused, however, of threatening the institution when he wanted the US to send delegates to a Pan American conference. Some of the delegates would be men of color, and for American delegates to meet with them like equals was alarming to southern politicians.[396]

Indeed, Adams' frequent framing of America's moral imperatives, coupled with the fact that he was the first northern, non-slaveholding president in years, was enough to make proslavery forces oppose him.[397] Thus, Adams received all the disadvantages of opposing slavery without any of the moral benefits of actually making a definitive abolitionist stand on the issue as president. Adams said he believed that when the war over slavery eventually arrived, "it will be my duty...to give my opinion."[398]

After Adams' unhappy, single term as president, he was chosen to represent Massachusetts in the House of Representatives. When Adams settled into the House, "he devoted his remarkable prestige and tireless energies to the struggle against slavery," wrote a future Massachusetts politician named John F. Kennedy.[399] Representative Adams focused first, though unsuccessfully, on keeping Texas out of the Union. He did so despite the fact that a victory on the issue would have meant slowing the growth of the United States across North

country in Adams' mind. He wrote in his diary on October 14, 1833 that slavery would "split up this Union." Charles Francis Adams, L 17.
[395] Edel, 205.
[396] Ibid., 222.
[397] Ibid., 247.
[398] Ibid., 251.
[399] Kennedy, 44.

America. Again, it was a genuine sacrifice for such a committed nationalist.[400] Also, it contradicts the writings of Kenneth O'Reilly who characterizes Adams as a man who just wanted the West and did not care who settled it, self-sufficient farmer or plantation owner.[401]

It not unsurprising that when Adams did decide to face slavery head on, he did so with an unconventional approach. He characterized the institution as being incompatible with democracy, which does not sound that creative until one notes that he argues that democracy for whites was what was really being undermined. Adams was concerned with the three-fifths compromise—the deal made at the constitutional convention that counted a slave as three-fifths of person when it came to determining states' populations (and thus their representation in Congress). This gave slave states a greater say in the House of Representatives than they should have had. Southern politicians were not representing the views of their slaves, but the slave population inflated the number of southern representatives. As a result, southern whites had more representation per capita than whites in free states. Worse yet, proslavery forces in Congress pushed through a gag rule that prevented even the discussion of abolitionist bills. The proslavery forces insisted that such talk trickled down to the slaves and helped foment rebellion. Adams argued that if members of Congress could be denied freedom of speech what protection was there for the rest of America?[402]

Adams still maintained a course of moderation. For example, he resisted supporting a movement that called for a quick end to slavery in Washington DC because he deemed it "utterly impracticable." And he never formally joined the abolitionist movement, but he was sympathetic and he passionately fought against the gag rule that sought to silence debate on the topic. It was this opposition to the attack on free speech that prompted Congress to censure him in 1837.[403]

Many in Congress liked the gag rule because it gave them an excuse to not argue about a topic that was so awkward, uncomfortable,

---

[400] Edel, 260.
[401] O'Reilly, 31.
[402] Edel, 265-267.
[403] Ibid., 269-270.

and seemingly intractable.[404] But by couching his opposition in terms of the right to petition—basically casting the gag rule as a threat to freedom of speech, which it was—Adams gained support for his position from thousands of northerners who had no great interest in abolition itself.[405]

Though not formally an abolitionist, Adams's work prompted Virginia Congressman Henry Wise to say that Adams was "the acutest, the astutest, (and) the archest enemy of southern slavery that ever existed."[406]

One reason that Adams was such a serious adversary of slavery was that he was willing to research and try to understand the proslavery position. He recorded in his diary in 1833 that he had read some of their literature arguing that slavery brought out the virtues of slave owners. Adams disagreed with the author's conclusions, but at least the former president knew what the arguments for the position were. It made his attacks more effective.[407]

Though he never called for an immediate, outright emancipation for American slaves, he did attack the pro-slavery position on many fronts. Perhaps the most famous example of this was his argument before the Supreme Court on behalf of the *Amistad* Africans.

The *Amistad* was a Spanish ship that had Africans on board intended for a life of slavery. The victims had taken over the ship, which subsequently drifted into American waters. The Africans were detained by American forces, but the would-be slaves had argued successfully in court that they should be freed. President Martin Van Buren challenged this decision, despite the fact that the international slave trade had already been outlawed here. Adams stood before the Supreme Court and argued for hours, citing among other things the Declaration of Independence that was hanging on the wall in the

[404] Norma Lois Peterson, *The Presidencies of William Henry Harrison & John Tyler* (Lawrence: University of Kansas, 1989), 5.
[405] William Dusinberre, *Slavemaster President* (New York: Oxford University Press, 2003), 123.
[406] Edel, 272.
[407] Charles Francis Adams, L 17.

courtroom. Adams won, sealing his place in history as an advocate for freedom.[408]

Adams' preparation for leadership was thorough in the extreme. When his father went to negotiate the treaty that ended the Revolutionary War, young John Quincy went along with him as his private secretary. John Quincy was only sixteen, and this was not even his first diplomatic trip to Europe. A few years earlier, he had served as a personal secretary and translator for the American diplomat to Russia.

Historian Joseph J. Ellis writes that one of George Washington's many strengths was his ability to recognize talent when he saw it. He picked Adams as a diplomat, and the choice was confirmed unanimously in the Senate.[409] The young man went on to serve in the diplomatic corps of John Adams and Madison, too. Thus, Quincy Adams served as a diplomat for both political parties and for the only nonpartisan president in American history. In fact, such was Adams' diplomatic prowess and leadership ability that Madison put him in charge of the American team that negotiated the end of the War of 1812. Adams also served as a US senator before spending eight years as Monroe's secretary of state, holding the same Cabinet office as the three presidents who served before him. Thus, one could make the argument that John Quincy Adams was better-prepared for the White House than any of his predecessors.

There was, however, a darker side to Adams and his background. His parents, as brilliant, patriotic, and loving as they were, arguably overwhelmed their child with their great expectations and their formula for his success. He was counseled by them to limit how much he laughed, and at age ten was writing to his father about being dissatisfied with himself when he "idled...away" time by playing games. Abigail Adams, as brilliant as she was, admonished her son in letters to pursue "excellence and morality" in the words of Edel, but what her correspondence too often lacked was love or warmth. As Edel puts it, "While he had been a talkative and charming youth, he seemed

---

[408] Edel, 283.
[409] Ellis, 160.

to be transforming into a young man of little social skill or grace."[410] Also, as stated in chapter four, John Quincy's father thought it strangely virtuous to support unpopular positions—this trait showed that the politician was not driven by the need for approval. The father transmitted this politically disadvantageous mindset to his son.

Louisa Adams was not oblivious to what she was getting when she married the man. Edel writes, "Her initial judgments of his extreme irritability, self-righteousness over matters of propriety, and volcanic temper were well founded." She would later be frustrated that his ambition often took precedence over what was best for their family. He was also arrogant, [411] which was all the more irritating to his enemies because he had many accomplishments to be arrogant about.

In the words of historian Joseph J. Ellis, John Quincy Adams "was not a happy man, lacked the emotional spontaneity of his father, and seemed to regard laughter as an unnatural act." Ellis theorizes that part of the problem was that Adams was so remarkably mature as a boy that he never enjoyed a true childhood. And how could he when his father had said, as mentioned earlier, that if Quincy Adams did not rise up to run the country, it was due to laziness and stubbornness? Ellis went on to note that father and son had "a conspicuous flair for alienating voters while acting in their long-term interest."[412]

The younger Adams was aware of his flaws, even if he was unable or unwilling to change them. By his own admission, he was "reserved, cold, and aloof." He readily acknowledged to his wife that he understood his personality problem, but he said, "I have not the pliability to reform it."[413]

He briefly served as a Massachusetts state senator, but he was so contentious in that role that in the words of Edel, Adams' colleagues "kicked him upstairs" to the United States Senate.[414] Predictably, Adams did not get along with his fellow Federalists in Washington DC either.

---

[410] Edel, 26-27, 33, 49.
[411] Edel, 103-104, 182.
[412] Ellis, 214.
[413] Edel, 52, 104, 296.
[414] Ibid., 90.

The Federalist Party was driven at this point to look out for the interests of the New England area, whereas Adams was a nationalist. When President Jefferson decided to cut off trade with Britain in response to British mistreatment of US shippers, Adams sided with the president. The trade embargo was brutal to the New England economy, but Adams thought it was necessary, so he supported the president's policy, even though his fellow Federalists were outraged by it and him.[415]

He wanted the country to grow, even if that meant growing in an area that was better for the future of the Democratic-Republican Party. Adams actually ended up resigning from the Senate in 1808 rather than waiting to be voted out of office. But staying true to his principles paid off. Because of his support for expansion (specifically the Louisiana Purchase), and the quality of his prior work as a diplomat, James Madison picked Adams to be the US Ambassador to Russia.[416]

When Madison's successor, James Monroe, chose Adams to serve as secretary of state, Adams stressed that his role was to serve the administration, not his own interests.[417] Adams was not oblivious to the fact that the last three presidents had served as secretaries of state before climbing to the top, but it is to the man's credit that he tried not to lose sight of his obligations to the chain of command. As noted in the last chapter, the same cannot be said for all of his fellow Cabinet members.

Adams was a positive force within the State Department. Some of the changes he made there proved useful all the way into the twentieth century.[418]

Adams had good role models as leaders. The younger Adams was so inspired by his father; the first president, whom Quincy Adams named a son after; and Jefferson, to whom Quincy Adams had grown so close when they both lived in France that it prompted John Adams to say to Jefferson, "He was as much your son as mine." John Quincy Adams wanted to be president, to truly live up to the level of these

---

[415] Kennedy, 38-41.
[416] Edel, 90-96.
[417] Ibid., 109.
[418] Ibid., 115-116.

men. But his father had handed him the quintessential Buddhist riddle: The need to attain without grasping. How does one gain the approval necessary to win elections without cultivating the popularity of the masses?[419] Charles Edel believes that Quincy Adams was inspired by the same source Ralph Ketcham wrote about in *Presidents above Party*. Ketcham's topic, again, was the idealized patriot king that Bolingbroke described. As mentioned throughout *Presidential Character*, this image of the virtuous ruler inspired all of the first six presidents. Edel believes that the impact of this inspiration on both father and son Adams was that they were obsessed with not looking like self-promoters.[420]

Quincy Adams' navigation of this road was neither easy nor pretty. His predecessor James Monroe believed that Adams was the most qualified man to be president, but Monroe also thought it was beneath the dignity of his office to openly advocate for a specific candidate to succeed him.[421] Adams suffered a light lapse in integrity, using his authority as secretary of state to offer several of his rivals in 1824 ambassadorial positions outside the country.[422] It was not his finest moment, but it is almost irrelevant since none of the men accepted his offers.

Generally speaking, though, Adams consistently avoided political games and partisan politics. Upon the completion of his presidency and election to the House of Representatives, he continued to be steadfast in this philosophy. Adams was asked to come out in support of the re-election bid of one of his colleagues. Adams replied that he liked the man in question, a General H.A.S. Dearborn, but Adams would not violate the decision he had made as president. Adams would not weigh in on any elections.[423]

After winning the presidency only when the House of Representatives settled the Election of 1824 by voting him in, Adams outlined an ambitious vision for the country that even his Cabinet did

---

[419] Edel, 192-194; Ellis, 114-115.
[420] Edel interview.
[421] Unger, 325.
[422] Edel, 199.
[423] He recorded this in his diary on July 21, 1833. Charles Francis Adams, L 6-7.

not support. As Adams biographer Charles N. Edel writes, "Political leadership was as much about pointing the way as it was about persuading others to follow." Edel restates this concern later in his study on the sixth president, writing that "while the vision Adams had sketched for his presidency was robust, his legislative strategy for translating it into policy was curiously weak." Adams was a top rate diplomat—he knew how to be persuasive and how to hammer out a decent compromise, but as president he seemed disinterested in persuasion or compromise. He laid out his arguments and expected the results to take care of themselves.[424]

Adams might have been blinded to outside perceptions because, ironically, he had seen the presidency so clearly. For example, his call for a national university, which could certainly be considered an example of federal government overreach since education is not in its constitutionally-authorized purview, was advocated by every president before him: Washington, the first Adams, and the three, states' rights-loving Democratic-Republicans that followed them.[425]

For limited-government Andrew Jackson supporters in Congress—who were already bitter that their man lost despite getting more votes than Adams—and to many in the country at large, proposals to get the government involved in science, education, and internal improvements were like adding insult to injury.[426] A conciliatory nod to Jacksonian sensibilities might have gone a long way, but a blueprint for bigger government was what Adams offered America.

It was all so thoroughly John Quincy Adams. He was remarkably smart, so he naturally valued a pursuit of scientific knowledge, and he wanted to improve education. As a committed nationalist, he wanted the country to grow, so internal improvements like roads and canals were necessary for communication, travel, and trade. And because he was a male Adams, he aggravated people so much that they did not want to see the logic of his position.

---

[424] Edel, 211, 213, 219, 235.
[425] Ralph Ketcham, *Presidents above Party* (Chapel Hill: University of North Carolina Press, 1984), 90-91.
[426] Sam W. Haynes, *James K. Polk* (New York: Pearson Longman, 2006), 22.

As Edel puts it, "While he did have some successes, by almost any account, including his own, his presidency was an abject failure."[427] Adams worked for years to be in the ultimate leadership position in America. He studied, and he prepared. He could have sought advice from several successful presidents before him, but instead relied on the advice of the one man who had been the least successful in the job—his father.

Yet, Quincy Adams' failure was not total. It was with quite some satisfaction that he assumed a seat in the House of Representatives after his home district sent him back to Washington. He wrote in his diary that "No election or appointment conferred upon me ever gave me so much pleasure."[428] His constituents knew he would not charm them, or even try to please them, but he would serve with integrity. He was infuriating, but he was incorruptible.

John Quincy Adams was a committed Bible reader and church attender, who did not hold an orthodox view of Christ. He never owned a slave, and struck blows against the institution, but he never formally joined an abolitionist group. Because of the slavery issue, he resisted some efforts to expand the nation's borders despite being a fervent nationalist. Finally, he was a gifted diplomat who badly wanted to be president, then he refused to behave diplomatically once he took office. In short, for all of his great talent, John Quincy Adams was a man of contradictions, and that reality frequently frustrated his agenda.

---

[427] Edel, 242.
[428] Kennedy, 45.

CHAPTER 9

CONCLUSION

All six men were tenacious in their efforts to impact the unfolding of the American story, but their styles were distinct. Where Washington was famously reserved, John Adams was passionate. Jefferson was relational but Machiavellian, whereas Madison was relational and collaborative. Monroe used traditions to bring people together, but John Quincy Adams rose to the top by being stubbornly contrarian.

Religion was part of the public discourse of all of these men, but its impact on their lives varied, as did their views on the subject. But how did their views stand up to Scripture? What follows is not an exhaustive biblical appraisal of these men, but it will provide some food for thought.

John Adams and his son were both quite religious, but their lack of belief in a Trinitarian view of God, which included a skepticism about the deity of Christ, puts them outside of orthodox Christianity. The senior Adams thought the concept of the Trinity was illogical, and the doctrine of salvation by faith alone was bad because it could "discourage the practice of virtue," as he wrote in his diary.[429] His most famous son agreed. Someone who did not agree was the Apostle Paul, who spent every chapter of Galatians arguing that humanity could never be good enough for Heaven, and the only means to salvation was, indeed, faith alone.

---

[429] Steven Waldman, *Founding Faith* (New York: Random House, 2008), 35.

George Washington believed that God intervened in the affairs of humanity. The first president also belonged to a church that espoused traditional Christian views. According to his biographer Ron Chernow, "That Washington believed in the need for good works as well as faith can be seen in his extensive charity."[430] Thus the first president lived out the admonitions found throughout the Book of James. Those who question the depth or particulars of Washington's faith frequently point out his lack of overt, public references to Jesus. However, given Washington's frequent participation in the oath-taking necessary to be both a vestryman and a godfather, the man did make public professions of faith in Christ over and over again. He just tended to not do that in political settings. Thus, based on his faith and works, it is easier to argue for rather than against the Christianity of Washington.

Madison might have been a Christian, too, according to Bishop Meade, and as possibly evidenced by some of Madison's personal habits later in life. Of course there is a biblical standard going back to Deuteronomy 17:6 that two or three witnesses is much more convincing than the testimony of just one. It is possible for a reasonable person to draw a conclusion in favor of Madison's Christianity, but it does require, well, a bit of a leap of faith. Except for church attendance, religious comments not uncommon for a politician, and an evangelical-sounding wartime letter to a friend, Madison's successor James Monroe shows little evidence of a deep faith. Both men struggle with the spiritual standard described in Matthew 7:16, which describes how people can be judged by their fruit. Does a lack of clear evidence in favor of faith tell the story for both of these men? Perhaps it does, though it might be a little easier to argue against Monroe's religiosity.

Finally, Thomas Jefferson thought that Jesus was a great moral teacher for other people, but that was about the extent of it. This falls short of what the fourth Gospel writer says in John 3:16 where belief in Christ is stated as a necessity for eternal life. John returns to this theme in the fourteenth chapter of his Gospel when he quotes Jesus as saying that no one gets to the Father without Christ.

---

[430] Ron Chernow *Washington* (New York: Penguin Books, 2011), 133.

When it came to their performance as presidents, these men were able to voice generic religious sentiments in a way that the public found at best to be comforting, and at least inoffensive. Even those who were less religious, like Monroe, could say the right things when necessary. The most controversial of them all, Jefferson, actually generated support among the pious with his championing of religious liberty. They all held to the position that the public good was served by the influence of the Christian religion because of its call to righteous behavior.[431] Thus, even though most of these presidents were not necessarily driven by the Christian faith in the performance of their jobs, they were respectful enough of traditional Christianity to make the voters, first in their local regions then on a national level, supportive.

Assessing the first six presidents on the slavery issue seems easier than it is. One would be tempted to say that the two men who did not own slaves were on the right side of the issue, and the slave owners were on the side of evil. At least one part of that equation is accurate. John Adams single-handedly opened the door to end slavery in Massachusetts with his writing of that state's constitution. John Quincy Adams fought the institution in the House of Representatives by attacking the gag rule that prevented debate over it, and he argued before the Supreme Court on behalf of a group of men and women who were otherwise destined for servitude.

The Virginians, of course, are in another category. They all had easier lives economically and socially because of the enforced labor of African Americans on their plantations. However, it does need to be pointed out that all four men were raised from birth in a culture that taught them that slavery was normal and good. It is to their credit that these future presidents were able to overcome an indoctrination that favored them and their kind. Washington, Jefferson, Madison, and Monroe were all able to see past the rhetoric and rationalizations.

---

[431] Once when Jefferson complained of having his religious views misrepresented, he argued that "The importance of religion to society has too many founded supports to need aid from imputations so entirely unfounded." J. Jefferson Looney, *The papers of Thomas* Jefferson, Volume 10 (Princeton: Princeton University Press, 2013), 394-395.

Washington realized that slavery was incompatible with the ideals of liberty that drove him to fight for his country's freedom. Despite being constricted within the limits of state law, Washington gradually made things better for his slaves and then freed them altogether in his will. Jefferson saw the morally corrupting influence of slavery and worked for its end, though he did essentially change course as he got older. Also, sadly, historian Robert Forbes writes that Jefferson's "denigration of the capacities of Africans probably exceeded most of his contemporaries."[432] Madison and Monroe both worked diligently for years on a plan that would help facilitate the end of slavery in the United States.

Could the four Virginians have done more to fight slavery? Yes, they could have. Did they do more to fight this injustice than most Americans of their day? Actually, they all did. Did they do more to fight an injustice in their midst than most Americans throughout our history? How much do most Americans do to fight injustice? Only about half of all eligible Americans even bother to vote on their political convictions once every four years. How many fewer do anything more than that?

Of course, such an argument threatens to let the Virginians off too easily. They did fight the injustice, but they did not defeat it, and in the mean time they benefitted from it.

If one defines leadership as the art of influencing people and/or events, the six men in this study provide many examples of how to do it. Washington became a leader by virtue of his integrity, cool reserve, and sheer physicality. Adams rose to the top thanks to his brilliance, hard work, ability as a public speaker, and, again, one sees personal integrity on display. Jefferson had an intellect that rivaled and possibly surpassed Adams, but the third president also had a charisma that John Adams could only dream of (and then Adams would have felt guilty for the vanity of such a dream). Madison's influence came from his brilliance—quite the recurring theme with these men—and also his

---

[432] Robert Pierce Forbes, *The Missouri Compromise and its Aftermath* (Chapel Hill: University of North Carolina Press, 2007), Kindle. L 596-603.

hard work at intellectual pursuits, but what made him unique as a leader was his gift for forming productive collaborative relationships with other great men, specifically Washington, Hamilton, and most famously Jefferson. Monroe's leadership ability came from his personal charm, which was second only to Jefferson's among these six men— Washington was popular, but he was not a charmer. Monroe also appealed strongly to the nostalgic impulses of Americans. Monroe's service in the Revolution, his old fashioned wardrobe selections, and the tour that he took—which echoed Washington's efforts—all would have brought a sense of comfort and familiarity to many Americans. Of course, it also helped Monroe's level of influence that the opposition party was collapsing as he was in the White House. John Quincy Adams rose to the top methodically. He served in nearly every possible office along the way.

It is worth noting that the flaws of these men were readily apparent. One hardly needs to be perfect to be a successful leader. Washington had a tendency to be too sensitive regarding his reputation.

Adams was so prickly he could not even get along with Ben Franklin. Also, for as brilliant as Adams was, he was not shrewd enough to surround himself with a loyal Cabinet.

Jefferson's character issues became a distraction when the Sally Hemings scandal broke. And, though Jefferson is typically praised for his use of words, even here he was not perfect. The man who once wrote that "The tree of liberty must be refreshed from time to time with the blood of tyrants and patriots," thought that the French Revolution was the natural next step to the American version. This might be considered a harmless sentiment, but Jefferson went on to say, "The liberty of the whole earth was depending on the issue of the contest, and…rather than it should have failed, I would have seen half the earth desolated."[433] Fortunately, it did not come to that.

Madison might have let events get away from him leading up the War of 1812. Instead of being a leader, Madison became a follower of more passionate politicians in Congress on this matter.

---

[433] Harlow Giles Unger, *The Last Founding* Father (Philadelphia: Da Capo Press, 2010), 95.

Monroe avoided rather than faced the slavery dispute impacting Missouri's statehood. Even if Monroe could not have single-handedly solved the country's biggest issue, weighing in on it would have been nice.

John Quincy Adams was ultimately undone as a leader by three things. One, his personality was so difficult that political allies lost their will to fight for him. Two, the only ex-president he took advice from was the only one to get voted out of office. Three, despite being a shrewd diplomat, he did not bother to be diplomatic with his fellow politicians when he was president.

One does find some overlap in the three areas of study in this book. If the religious values of these men shaped their attitudes towards slavery, only two of them made it clear in these pages. Monroe commented that God had made both races, encouraging sensitive handling of slaves based on that. John Quincy Adams said slavery violated the Christian principles of the United States. They all applied their leadership skills to the problem of slavery. Though they could not constitutionally come up with an end to it, they all attacked it on some level for at least a portion of their professional careers. They did not just bemoan its reality, and they were not simply defined by what they could not do. They could not all claim credit for eradicating it in an entire state, like the second president did in Massachusetts, but they did push against it. And that is leadership.

These six men all had their share of flaws, but each of them was great in some way, or they never would have gained enough admiration from their peers to become presidents. In vastly different ways, and despite their imperfections, these men were giants.

Appendix: Sources

A book like *Presidential Character* obviously requires many sources. Primary documents were particularly useful, but biographies, topical works, and interviews also proved quite helpful. For those interested in learning more about the first six presidents, what follows in this section is a look at some of the sources that were used.

Several primary sources were available. Most of them are pretty straightforward collections of the important papers of the early presidents, but there are some works that are worth specific mention. The book labeled *John Adams Autobiography* does not tell his full story, but it does cover significant portions of his political career roughly around the time of the American Revolution. Bishop William Meade's *Old Churches, Ministers, and Families of Virginia* is a collection of information about and reflections on prominent Virginians that was first published in the middle of the 1800s. It is significant because Meade offers some early insights on the Virginians who became presidents. Despite Meade's Episcopalian connection with these men, he does not color all of them with the same brush. John Marshall's *The Life of George Washington* should be considered a primary document because Marshall was a contemporary of the first president. Marshall was actually the first Chief Justice of the Supreme Court, and he gives the reader a firsthand account of how Washington was perceived by one who knew him personally. A final primary source worth mentioning is the *Memoirs of John Quincy Adams*. Like the *John Adams Autobiography*, this collection, too, was edited by Charles Francis Adams, who was a son of John Quincy. Unfortunately, the Kindle version of The *Memoirs of John Quincy Adams* only starts in 1833, several years after the end of the sixth president's term. Happily, a complete version of the writings is available at www.masshist.org.

Some of the works cited in *Presidential Character* actually fall into multiple categories. For example, Mary V. Thompson's book, *In the Hands of a Good Providence: Religion in the Life of George Washington*, provides an overview of Washington's life, but it also explores his faith in great detail. Another example of a book fitting multiple needs, and perhaps the most perfect resource for *Presidential Character*, is Charles N. Edel's biographical work, *Nation Builder: John Quincy Adams and the Grand Strategy of the Republic*. Edel looks at Adams' moral/spiritual framing of the potential of the United States, which gives the reader insight into the religious outlook of the sixth president. Edel's treatment of Adams' "grand strategy" says something about Adams' leadership philosophy, and Edel also covers in detail the evolution of Adams' fight against slavery. It was as if Edel wrote his book with *Presidential Character* in mind.

Harlow Giles Unger's *The Last Founding Father* provides a great look at the fifth president while also characterizing the fourth. Unger's work is interesting, and well-researched, but he does sometimes engage in overly harsh language. Examples of his characterizations of Madison are seen earlier in *Presidential Character*. To demonstrate that the rhetoric aimed at Madison might be a little excessive, it is helpful to note another one of Unger's characterizations. Unger records the words of Louisa Adams, the wife of the sixth president, describing how even when she and other women dress up, "we are certain of being eclipsed by the Sovereign Lady of the mansion (Mrs. Monroe)." Was there sarcasm here by Mrs. Adams?[434] Maybe there was. On the other hand, maybe there was not; it is tricky to decipher tone in a personal letter almost two hundred years after the fact. But as Unger describes it, Louisa Adams "caterwauled."[435] That does not quite seem fair.

---

[434] Or in modern parlance, "snarkiness?"
[435] Harlow Giles Unger, *The Last Founding Father* (Philadelphia: Da Capo, 2010), 324.

Another unique biography is the one on James Madison by Lynne Cheney.[436] It's not just that it is an interesting work, but it is intriguing to read about Madison from the point of view of someone who is not just a prolific author, but also the wife of a former vice president.

By the time I got to Ron Chernow's Pulitzer Prize winning *Washington: A Life*, I already had ample material on the first president, but Chernow's insights on Washington's faith were so intriguing, I had to include some of them.

Our understanding of the religious views of the presidents is obscured by a problem mentioned in the Introduction. Books are limited by the biases of those who care enough to research their topic and share their findings. As Alf J. Mapp, Jr. so aptly puts it when talking about the first president, "Many writers have tended to interpret Washington's views on religion in terms of their own predilections."[437] On one side of the argument, there are evangelical preachers and other Christian writers who tend to overstate the religiosity of the Founders. On the other side, there are equally aggressive secularist academicians who look at the same men and only see Deists. David L. Holmes alludes to this when discussing the first president specifically, "Evangelical...authors tend to find orthodoxy and zeal in Washington's religion. Professional historians, however, find the chain of evidence supporting Washington's exemplary piety weak."[438] Jon Meacham makes virtually the same point with the third president, saying "The right would like Jefferson to be a soldier of faith, the left an American Voltaire."[439]

The evangelical authors do not try to obscure their goals, but they do offer interesting arguments. One prominent member of this

---

[436] Lynne Cheney, *James Madison: A Life Reconsidered* (New York: Viking Books, 2014).

[437] Alf J. Mapp, Jr., *The Faiths of our Founders* (New York: Fall River Press, 2006), 67.

[438] David L. Holmes, *The Faiths of the Founding Fathers* (New York: Oxford University Press, 2006), 69.

[439] Jon Meacham, *American Gospel* (New York: Random House, 2007), 4.

camp is Tim LaHaye who made a name for himself as a pastor, marriage expert, and author of books on eschatology. What established LaHaye as a nationally known figure, though, was his *Left Behind* series of novels that he co-authored with Jerry Jenkins. In short, LaHaye is not an academically-recognized scholar of historical American Christianity, but that does not stop him from weighing in on the subject. In LaHaye's book *Faith of our Founding Fathers*, he argues that there is evidence of a considerable amount of Christian belief and practice among the forefathers, but he does acknowledge that this faith was not held universally among them.

David Barton is a hero among a portion of evangelicals, but he stands accused of putting a too-Christianized slant on American history. His book, *The Jefferson Lies: Exposing the Myths You've Always Believed about Thomas Jefferson*, argues among other things that Jefferson was a type of Christian who supported equality for African Americans and did not really edit out the miracles of the Bible because of his personal skepticism.[440] Frankly, as is demonstrated in *Presidential Character*, history is not on Barton's side. Even his fellow evangelical LaHaye takes Jefferson's unorthodox views on Christianity for granted.[441] Contrasts to Barton are also provided by Garry Will's *Negro President: Jefferson and the Slave Power*, which highlights Jefferson's perspectives on slavery[442] and Joseph J. Ellis' book *American Sphinx: The Character of Thomas Jefferson*.

Robert W. Pelton is another unabashed evangelical writer. His book *George Washington's Prophetic Vision* is even subtitled *A Uniquely Different Piece of American History*. Pelton makes an interesting case when he quotes a relative of the first president who took the man's orthodoxy for granted, but Pelton is on shakier ground when he retells stories that have had their credibility questioned.[443]

Closer to the middle of the spectrum, we have Steven Waldman, author of *Founding Faith*. Waldman describes George Washington as a

---

[440] David Barton, *The Jefferson Lies* (Nashville: Thomas Nelson, 2012), Kindle.
[441] Tim LaHaye, *Faith of Our Founding Fathers* (Master Books, 1994), 2828, Kindle.
[442] Garry Wills, *Negro President* (Boston: Houghton Mifflin, 2003), 8-9.
[443] Robert W. Pelton, *George Washington's Prophetic* Vision (West Conshohocken, PA: Infinity Publishing Company, 2007), 9, 12, 37.

man who does not take Communion, encourages religious tolerance (as if to say this makes Washington theologically indifferent), and makes few references if any to the deity of Christ. Waldman thus concludes that the first president was most likely a Unitarian. Waldman, though, acknowledges that there are those to the left of him who would portray almost all of the Founders as Deists or secularists.[444]

Nixon's Piano by Kenneth O'Reilly offers an overview of all the US presidents and their treatment of the race issue from Washington through Bill Clinton. The book is an interesting and helpful resource, though, ironically, it seems a little biased. According to the jacket to the book, every single president O'Reilly wrote about sacrificed African American interests for their own political gain except for Lincoln and Lyndon Johnson. That is a little harsh. Certainly some, and arguably many, presidents have been personally or politically biased, but the presidents have also been limited and/or pressured by constitutional and political realities. Also, some of the characterizations are unfair. For example, O'Reilly's belief that John Q. Adams cared more about business interests than the evils of slavery greatly misrepresents the New Englander.[445]

Robert Pierce Forbes's book, *The Missouri Compromise and its Aftermath*, provided a great portrait of Americans' views on slavery up to and through 1820. It also provides interesting insight regarding Monroe. That said, there were a couple of issues that arose in the reading. Forbes identified the childhood teacher of Washington, Madison, and Monroe as Archibald Campbell, a Presbyterian parson. It seems unlikely that these Anglican families of early eighteenth century Virginia would have gone to Campbell if he was not a fellow Anglican. Also, Forbes writes that Monroe "remained in public service without a break" from the Revolution until he left the White House,[446] but Monroe actually did have a break from public service before the end of Jefferson's presidency and through the beginning of Madison's time in

---

[444] Steven Waldman, *Founding Faith* (New York: Random House, 2008), 56-63, 193.
[445] Kenneth O'Reilly, *Nixon's Piano* (New York: The Free Press, 1995), 31.
[446] Robert Pierce Forbes, *The Missouri Compromise and its Aftermath* L (Chapel Hill: University of North Carolina Press, 2007), 352.

the White House.[447] Despite such nitpicking, overall Forbes' work is an interesting and worthwhile book.

It would not make much sense to write about leadership and the early presidents without referencing Richard Brookhiser's *George Washington on Leadership*. Though the book was written primarily for the business world, the historical references are first rate. Another nice feature of this work is that as Brookhiser makes his points, he frequently shares relevant tidbits about other presidents.

Robert M. Johnstone, Jr. has some interesting things to say about Jefferson's leadership and its impact on the presidency, though the overall effectiveness of the book might be limited somewhat by the author's sympathy for the third president.[448] Or, perhaps I am limited in my appreciation for the book due to my hostility to Jefferson.

Jon Meacham does a valiant job of trying to paint a generally positive picture of the third president in *Thomas Jefferson: The Art of Power*. Meacham argues that part of the negativity towards Jefferson stems from recent books on Washington, John Adams, and even Alexander Hamilton. In the process of extolling the virtues of these men, biographers have cast Jefferson in a more negative light. Meacham concedes, though, that the DNA evidence linking Jefferson to Sally Hemings' children did not do Jefferson's reputation any favors either.[449] Meacham is almost convincing, but his portrayal of Jefferson's flaws is too thorough to fully accept Meacham's premise. Nevertheless, the book is a helpful look at Jefferson, especially because of its focus on Jefferson's use of power, which says a lot about his approach to leadership.

Presidents above Party by Ralph Ketcham is a great resource because it talks about the vision the first six presidents had for the presidency. It makes sense to know what they were trying to accomplish before completely judging what they actually did.

---

[447] Unger (2009), 202-207.
[448] Robert M. Johnstone, Jr., *Jefferson and the Presidency* (Ithaca: Cornell University Press, 1978).
[449] Jon Meacham, *Thomas Jefferson* (New York: Random House, 2012), 507.

Finally, the people interviewed were most gracious with their time and insights. Randall O'Brien had some interesting things to say about leadership. W. Brian Shelton provided an expert's definitions of Christianity and some of its offshoots. Mary V. Thompson shared further insights into Washington, his faith, and Anglicanism in Virginia, and Charles N. Edel gave substantive opinions on Adams, Monroe, and Quincy Adams.

There are of course many other works that were cited, but this section was intended to provide the reader with a slightly deeper understanding of a cross section of the sources used.

Sources

Interviews

Edel, Charles N. Author of *Nation Builder: John Quincy Adams and the Grand Strategy of the Republic*. April 7, 2015.
O'Brien, Randall. President of Carson-Newman University, April 21, 2015.
Shelton, W. Brian, Provost of Toccoa falls College, April 19, 2015.
Thompson, Mary V. Author of *In the Hands of a Good Providence: Religion in the Life of George Washington*. March 26, 2015.

Bibliography

Primary Sources

Adams, Charles Francis, Editor. *John Adams Autobiography*. Amazon Digital Services, 1850. Kindle.
Adams, Charles Francis, Editor. *Memoirs of John Quincy Adams,* Kindle.
Adams, John Quincy. *Diary of John Quincy Adams*. www.masshist.org, Accessed 11/27/2015.
Fitzpatrick, John C., Editor. *The Writings of George Washington from the Original Manuscript Sources*. Volume 1, 1754-1756. Washington DC: US Printing Office, 1931.
Graham, Judith S., Beth Luey, Margaret A. Hogan, and James Taylor, Editors. *The Adams Papers: Diary and Autobiographical Writings of Louisa Catherine Adams*, Volume 2, 1819-1849.

Cambridge: MA: Belknap Press, 2013.

Hunt, John Gabriel. *The Inaugural Addresses of the Presidents.* Revised and Updated. New York: Gramercy Books, 2003.

Jefferson, Thomas. *Memoir, Correspondence, and Miscellanies from the papers of Thomas Jefferson (Complete)*, Edited by Thomas Jefferson Randolph. Alexandria, VA: The Library of Alexandria, 2008.

--------. *Notes on the State of Virginia.* Kindle.

Looney, J. Jefferson, Editor. *The Papers of Thomas Jefferson*, Volume 1, 4 March to 15 November 1809. Princeton, NJ: Princeton University Press, 2004.

---------. *The Papers of Thomas Jefferson*, Volume 9, 1 September 1815 to 30 April 1816. Princeton, NJ: Princeton University Press, 2012.

---------. *The Papers of Thomas Jefferson*, Volume 10, 1 May 1816 to 18 January 1817. Princeton, NJ: Princeton University Press, 2013.

Madison, James. *A Compilation of the Messages and Papers of the Presidents,* Volume 1, Part 4, Editor James D. Richardson (FQ Books, 2010), Kindle.

Marshall, John. *The Life of George Washington.* Edwards Publishing House, January 1, 2011. Kindle.

Meade, Bishop William. *Old Churches, Ministers, and Families of Virginia.* Philadelphia: J.B. Lippincott and Co., 2011. Kindle.

Monroe, James. *A Compilation of the Messages and Papers of the Presidents,* Volume 2, Part 1, Editor James D. Richardson (FQ Books, 2006), Kindle.

Rhodehamel, John. Editor, *Washington: Writings.* New York: The Library of America, 1997.

Shuffclton, Frank, Editor. *The Letters of John and Abigail Adams.* New York: Penguin Books, 2004.

Smith, James Morton Editor. *The Republic of Letters: The Correspondence between Thomas Jefferson and James Madison.* New York: W.W. Morton and Company, 1995.

Secondary Sources

Ahlstrom, Sydney E. *A Religious History of the American People*,
    Volumes 1 & 2. Garden City, NY: Image Books, 1975.
Barton, David. *The Jefferson Lies: Exposing the Myths You've always
    believed about Thomas Jefferson*. Nashville: Thomas Nelson,
    2012. Kindle.
Broadwater, Jeff. *James Madison: A Son of Virginia and a Founder of
    the Nation*. Chapel Hill: University of North Carolina Press,
    2012.
Brookhiser, Richard. *George Washington on Leadership*. New York:
    Perseus Book Group, 2009.
Cheney, Lynne. *James Madison: A Life Reconsidered*. New York:
    Viking, 2014.
Chernow, Ron. *Washington: A Life*. New York: Penguin Books, 2011.
Cullen, Jim. *Imperfect Presidents*. New York: Fall River Press, 2007.
Dusinberre, William. *Slavemaster President: The Double Career of
    James Polk*. New York: Oxford University Press, 2003.
Edel, Charles N. *Nation Builder: John Quincy Adams and the Grand
    Strategy of the Republic*. Cambridge, MA: Harvard University
    Press, 2014.
Ellis, Joseph J. *American Sphinx: The Character of Thomas Jefferson*.
    New York: Vintage Books, 1998.
------ *First Family*. New York: Vintage Books, 2010.
------ *Found Brothers: The Revolutionary Generation*. New York:
    Vintage Books, 2000.
------ *His Excellency: George Washington*. New York: Alfred A.
    Knopf, 2004.
Federer, William J., *America's God and Country: Encyclopedia of
    Quotations*. St. Louis: Amerisearch, 2000.
Forbes, Robert Pierce. *The Missouri Compromise and its Aftermath:
    Slavery & the Meaning of America*. Chapel Hill, 2007
Haynes, Sam W. *James K. Polk and the Expansionist Impulse*, third
    edition. New York: Pearson Longman, 2006.
Heyrman, Christine Leigh. *Southern Cross: The Beginning of the Bible
    Belt*. Chapel Hill: University of North Carolina Press, 1998.

Holmes, David. *The Faiths of the Founding Fathers*. New York:
    Oxford University Press, 2006.
Isaac, Rhys. *The Transformation of Virginia*. Chapel Hill: University of
    North Carolina, Press, 1982.
Johnstone, Jr., Robert M. *Jefferson and the Presidency: Leadership in
    the Young Republic*. Ithaca: Cornell University Press, 1978.
Ketcham, Ralph. *Presidents above Party: The First American
    Presidency, 1789-1829*. Chapel Hill: University of North
    Carolina Press, 1984.
LaHaye, Tim. *Faith of our Founding Fathers*. Master Books, January
    1, 1994. Kindle.
Langguth, AJ. *Patriots: The Men who started the American Revolution*.
    New York: Touchstone, 1989.
Leibiger, Stuart. *Founding Friendship: George Washington, James
    Madison, and the Creation of The American Republic*.
    Charlottesville: University of Virginia Press, 2001.
Levy, Andrew. *The First Emancipator: Slavery, Religion, and the
    Quiet Resolution of Robert Carter*. New York: Random House,
    2005.
Lillback, Peter A. with Jerry Newcombe. *George Washington's Sacred
    Fire*. Bryn Mawr, PA: Providence Forum Press, 2006.
Mapp, Jr., Alf J. *The Faith of our Fathers: What America's Founders
    Really Believed*. New York: Fall River Press, 2006.
Marshall, Peter, and David Manuel. *From Sea to Shining Sea: God's
    Plan for America Unfolds*. Grand Rapids: MI, 1986.
Mathews, Donald G. *Religion in the Old South*. Chicago: University of
    Chicago Press, 1979.
Meacham, Jon. *American Gospel: God, the Founding Fathers, and the
    Making of a Nation*. New York: Random House, 2007.
----- *Thomas Jefferson: The Art of Power*. New York: Random House,
    2012.
McCullough, David. *John Adams*. New York: Touchstone Books,
    2002.
Morgan, Edmund S. *American Slavery—American Freedom*. New
    York: W.W. Norton & Company, 1975.
Nelson, John K. *A Blessed Company: Parishes, Parsons, and*

Parishioners in Anglican Virginia, 1690-1776. Chapel Hill: University of North Carolina Press, 2002.

O'Reilly, Kenneth. *Nixon's Piano: Presidents and Racial Politics from Washington of Clinton.* New York: Free Press, 1995.

Parsons, Lynn Hudson. *The Birth of Modern Politics: Andrew Jackson, John Quincy Adams and the Election of 1828.* New York: Oxford University Press, 2009.

Pelton, Robert W. *George Washington's Prophetic Vision: A Uniquely Different Piece of American History.* West Conshohocken, PA: Infinity Publishing, 2006.

Peterson, Norma Lois. *The Presidencies of William Henry Harrison & John Tyler.* Lawrence: University of Kansas, 1989.

Seigenthaler, John. *James K. Polk.* New York: Henry Holt and Company, 2004.

Thompson, Mary V. *In the Hands of a Good Providence: Religion in the Life of George Washington.* Charlottesville: University of Virginia Press, 2008.

Unger, Harlow Giles. *The Last Founding Father: James Monroe and a Nation's Call to Greatness.* Philadelphia: Da Capo Press, 2010.

Waldman, Steven. *Founding Faith: Providence, Politics, and the Birth of Religious Freedom in America.* New York: Random House, 2008.

Weisberger, Bernard A. *America Afire: Jefferson, Adams, and the Revolutionary Election of 1800.* New York: William Morrow, 2000.

Wills, Garry. *"Negro President": Jefferson and the Slave Power.* Boston: Houghton Mifflin, 2003.

Index of Historical Figures

Abdee, Phoebe, 57
Adams, Abigail, 35, 53-55, 57
Adams, John, 12-13, 16-17, 21, 28-29, 35, 46, 51-67, 69, 71, 73, 75, 77-79, 81-82, 94, 96, 109, 111-112, 120-124, 126, 128-130, 132, 137-138
Adams, John Quincy, 16-17, 19, 28, 60-61, 76, 81-82, 94, 108-109, 111-126, 128, 130-133, 136, 138
Adams, Louisa, 114-115, 121, 133
Burwell, Rebecca Lewis, 80
Calhoun, John C., n. 10, 109, 115-116
Callender, James, 63, 77
Carter, Robert, 16, 21, 30-31
Clay, Henry, 109
Coles, Edward, 91
Cosway, Maria, 80
Crawford, William C., 109
Franklin, Ben, 21-22, 31, 51-52, 60, 65, 75, 93, 111, 130
Greene, Nathanael, 48
Hamilton, Alexander, n. 10, 49, 62-63, 97, 129, 137
Hemings, Sally, 67, 80, 130, 137
Henry, Patrick, 68, 92, 104
Jefferson, Martha (Patty), 99
Jefferson, Thomas, 13-14, 16-17, 27, 31-32, 37-38, 41-42, 46, 49, 51-56, 59, 63-85, 88-89, 92-96, 99-100, 105-106, 108-109, 111, 121-122, 126-130, 134-137
Lee, Henry, 50
Lewis, Eleanor Parke Custis, 42-45
L'Ouverture, Toussaint, 58
Madison, Dolley, 86-87, 90-91
Madison, James, 13, 16-17, 27, 31, 41, 49, 59, 64, 68, 74, 78, 81-96, 98, 100, 104-109, 111, 120, 122, 126-134, 136
Marshall, John, 41, 52, 98, 107, 132
McHenry, James, 63
Monroe, Elizabeth, 98, 105, 133
Monroe, James, 13, 16-18, 31, 36, 77, 88, 92, 95-111, 115, 120, 122-123, 126-131, 136, 138
Paine, Thomas, 46, 54, 70, 77
Walker, Elizabeth, 80
Washington, George, 11-12, 14-18, 27, 35-53, 58-59, 61-62, 64-65, 69, 71, 73-74, 77-79, 82, 86-89, 91, 93-94, 96, 98, 100, 104-109, 111-113, 115, 120, 124-130, 132-138
Washington, Martha, 44-45, 48

48554222R00081

Made in the USA
Lexington, KY
05 January 2016